THE
GRAIN-FREE
FAMILY TABLE

THE
GRAIN-FREE
FAMILY TABLE

125 DELICIOUS RECIPES FOR FRESH, HEALTHY EATING EVERY DAY

carrie vitt

WILLIAM MORROW

An Imprint of HarperCollins*Publishers*

HarperCollins books may be purchased for educational, business, or sales promotional use. For information please e-mail the Special Markets Department at SPsales@harpercollins.com.

FIRST EDITION

Designed by Kris Tobiassen of Matchbook Digital
Food photography by Carrie Vitt
Lifestyle photography by Kelly Trimble and Dede Edwards Photography
Photograph on page 77 courtesy of Corbin Gurkin (used with permission)

Library of Congress Cataloging-in-Publication Data has been applied for.

ISBN 978-0-06-230815-3

14   15   16   17   18   ID/QG   10   9   8   7   6   5   4   3   2   1

To my daughters, Hannah and Abby

The Lord blessed me beyond measure when he brought
you both into my life. Thank you for walking through this
grain-free journey with your dad and me. We are both so
proud of the sweet young ladies you've become!

contents

introduction

MY STORY

A simple trip to the dentist changed my life. In the spring of 2008 I went to the dentist because of a cracked amalgam filling in one of my teeth. The dentist removed the filling without taking proper precautions, and afterward I felt terrible. I spent nearly a week in bed recuperating—no easy task with two small daughters to raise. I thought my reaction to the removal was strange, but after a week I regained my strength and got on with my life.

A few weeks later, however, I began to have problems with my complexion, including breakouts, rough skin, and splotchy patches on my face. I hadn't changed anything in my daily regimen, I was on a diet of unprocessed organic foods, and I exercised regularly. I was confused. Months later, things got worse when I broke out in inexplicable hives from the neck up. My face was swollen and red, peeled twice a day, and felt like someone was holding a frying pan to my skin. I began eliminating things from my diet as I searched for a cause, but no change made a difference. I went to several doctors and they all told me I had dry skin, gave me a tube of steroid cream, and sent me on my way. I'm not an idiot. I knew my skin wasn't "dry," and I knew I had to dig deeper.

The hives continued to worsen by the day. One morning, I woke up and splashed some water on my face. Immediately, my face turned bright red and starting swelling and burning. "Oh no!" I thought. "It's the water!" I believed the chlorine in the water was making me sick. I told my husband and we tried to figure out our options. In the meantime I couldn't touch tap water, let alone drink it. We bought large bottles of filtered water and I sponge bathed for more than a month. I couldn't even wash my hands in tap water or I would start to swell and burn. We tried several unsuccessful solutions, but eventually bought a reverse osmosis water filtration system for the entire house. It wasn't cheap, but it helped. For the first time in more than a month, I could finally bathe again. My symptoms began to clear a little, but after a few weeks they came back. Worse. Much worse.

I cried. I became very depressed. I didn't want to go anywhere because not only did I look horrible, but I was in constant pain. I slept with ice packs on my face to ease the burning. I had to drop all my outside commitments, and I didn't get out to see my friends. I had become allergic to *everything*. If I ate vegetables, I would swell. If I ate meat, I would swell. If I walked into a room with too much perfume, I would swell. So I stayed at home. All day. Every day.

After six miserable months, I still didn't know what was causing the hives. No matter what I ate, drank, or did, I constantly had hives. I finally found a doctor who listened, and he sent me to an allergist. She did all the skin testing, but every test came back negative. Perplexed, she told me about an autoimmune disease that in some extreme cases causes hives, so she did a blood test for the antibodies. The test showed my immune system was attacking my thyroid gland. I was diagnosed with Hashimoto's disease. The doctor told me to start a thyroid medication, but after some research, I learned the medication would only calm the symptoms and not stop the formation of antibodies. I decided to look for an alternative solution.

One of my best friends, Karin, who patiently listened to me crying each day on the phone, told me about her sister Kim, a certified nutritionist. I called Kim and told her everything that was going on. She agreed to work with me. Remember the cavity I had removed and refilled? After many tests, we discovered my thyroid had absorbed most of the heavy metals from the amalgam filling and consequently caused my liver to "back up" so that it couldn't properly filter any toxins my body encountered. This helped explain the hives and the thyroid disease. The first thing Kim told me to do was drop all sugar, alcohol, meat, grains, fruit, dairy, and gluten. I was allowed only vegetables and healthy fats such as raw butter, duck fat, lard, coconut oil, and so on. It sounds drastic, but I had suffered for so long that I was willing to try anything. She also prescribed whole-food supplements and cleanses to begin the healing process.

So there I was writing a cooking blog, but I couldn't really cook. I felt as if my main creative outlet had been blocked. I didn't know there was a world of "grain-free" cooking and baking, so I ate vegetables. My husband, Pete, and the kids were gracious enough to eat the same diet. Pete said, "If you have to do this, then we'll do it together."

I couldn't go out to eat or eat at friends' homes. We traveled that summer, and I had to pack *all* my food in a cooler. We were gone for three weeks. It wasn't easy. I sponge bathed with filtered water. I think I may have offended friends along the way when I couldn't eat the food they provided. I tried to explain as I pulled dinner out of my cooler, but I wasn't sure they really understood. I could understand—I'd never heard of such a thing myself before it happened to me.

Avoiding gluten and grains was a very new thing for me. I mourned the fact that I couldn't bake or eat any of the favorite foods I'd grown up eating. It sounds silly now, but one night I actually cried because I thought I'd never be able to eat a cinnamon roll again or dredge chicken in flour.

Another symptom of Hashimoto's is that the thyroid hormone levels that control your metabolism can swing from high to low. So even though I was consistently working out during this time, I had months when my metabolism slowed and I would gain weight, and months when it would swing the other way and I'd lose weight. It was very frustrating, to say the least.

November of 2009 was my last hives attack. By Thanksgiving I was truly thankful—my skin was clear for the first time in a year. I passed on the rolls and breads because I still didn't know how to work with grain-free flours.

When I first began a grain-free diet I didn't know what ingredients to bake with, so I called a friend and she told me that nut flours are a great alternative. I bought these new-to-me flours and looked online for recipes, but I couldn't find any that tasted just like the breads, cookies, and cakes I loved. This was disappointing at first, but I was determined. I decided to experiment on my own. I learned that each flour has its own characteristics, and it's best to combine flours to achieve the necessary structure and integrity. I also found that unflavored gelatin is a fabulous binder for these gluten-free ingredients. Soon I created dozens of recipes for muffins, cakes, and cookies and took them to my neighbors, who taste-tested them for me. None of them ever guessed that my baked goods were made with grain-free flours. Bingo! I knew I was onto something, so I shared my ideas and recipes with my readers, and they came back with rave reviews.

I now eat a completely grain-free diet, and my disease is in remission. I have enjoyed finding ways to work with so many new ingredients. Despite the challenges, I can honestly say I'm thankful for the hardships I encountered. I now understand what it's like to have to avoid certain foods. I have much more empathy for people who suffer from ailments and can't find the answers. I now have a variety of grain-free flours and other ingredients at my fingertips. My experience was extreme, but it led me to answers that can help people facing a wide variety of health problems. I know many of you have Hashimoto's, celiac, allergies, diabetes, or other autoimmune diseases and have felt a sense of despair. I'm here to encourage you and tell you there *are* solutions. The foods we eat play a huge role in how our bodies work and heal, and there are many foods out there that can help you start the healing process. You *can*

move to a grain-free diet and enjoy delicious food. I want this book to be a practical guide so you, too, can find healing through food.

HOW I HEALED MYSELF

"I'm going to reverse the disease." This was my reply to the doctor when he told me my thyroid would eventually stop working and I'd be on medication for the rest of my life. I had already seen firsthand how food could make a difference in my health when I overcame chronic migraines, irritable bowel syndrome (IBS), and eczema with an organic, nutrient-dense diet, so I decided I would find a way to use food to reverse this disease as well. So what did I do? I did everything my nutritionist told me to do, no matter how difficult. This was a marathon, not a quick fix, but I was willing to take the challenge.

I know each body is different. I share this information to give you an overview of what I did to reverse *my* autoimmune disease. The protocol I followed was specifically tailored to my health needs. Finding a good nutritionist or holistic-minded, experienced health practitioner who can give you a specialized treatment plan for your body is crucial.

My Path to Healing

For the first thirty days I avoided all foods except vegetables and healthy saturated fats (see page 11). My nutritionist, Kim, told me that not all people need this level of restriction, but my system needed a chance to calm down, so eliminating almost everything was the right place to start.

After thirty days, I added raw dairy (made from unpasteurized milk) and organic, pastured meat back into my diet. I also drank homemade bone broth throughout the day. I ate some fermented foods at each meal; these included things like traditionally prepared sauerkraut (see page 258) and kimchi. I gave up *all* processed foods, soy, and grains.

Here are the foods I was allowed to eat:

Organic, pastured meats

Raw butter

Coconut oil

Ghee

Lard and tallow

Raw cheese

Cultured, organic dairy

Bone broth

Eggs

Vegetables

Fruit

Seeds

Nuts

Honey (in strict moderation)

Maple syrup (in strict moderation)

Coconut sugar (in strict moderation)

Here are the foods I removed from my diet:

All processed foods

Soy (except for small amounts of raw, fermented soy called Nama shoyu)

Grains

All GMO foods

The first months of following this diet were not easy, and the hives did not go away immediately. This was frustrating at times, but I knew I had to persevere. It took nine months of disciplined eating and cleansing before the hives disappeared com-pletely. That was a joyful day! But I still had a long way to go to reach complete healing. It took four and a half years of disciplined eating to achieve normal blood levels again, but I stuck with the plan and accomplished what the doctors said was impossible. At the end of my journey I felt like a new woman—full of energy, with vibrant skin and a new lease on life.

Supplements and Drainage Therapies

I took different whole-food supplements to help support my system and slowly begin the detox pro-cess. I particularly liked supplements from Standard Process and Biotics. My nutritionist's prescriptions for these supplements varied as my blood levels changed and my body healed.

We used several different drainage therapies from Unda to drain different organs in order to bring them back to vitality. I highly recommend ask-ing your practitioner about these therapies as they are gentle on the body and very effective. It is im-portant that your practitioner has been trained in the proper use of these remedies.

I took these basic supplements, which most people will find beneficial whether or not they have health issues:

Green Pastures fermented cod liver oil

GutPro probiotics

Pure Radiance vitamin C

I used these detox and cleansing methods:

Dry sauna—I spent twenty to twenty-five minutes in the dry sauna three times a week. The sauna helps remove toxins from the body, and I also found it very relaxing.

Dry brushing—Dry brushing can assist the body in removal of toxins and improve circulation, so I did this each evening before going to bed. A soft bristle body brush is brushed in a circular motion on the skin. It's an economical and easy way to support the lymphatic system and help the body detox.

Castor oil packs—I treated the thyroid and liver several times a week with a cleansing castor oil pack. When placed on the body, the oil is absorbed into the lymphatic circulation.

Long walks—My body couldn't handle intense workouts (I would be in bed for days if I overextended myself), so long walks were a gentle way to exercise and allow the lymphatic system to flush out.

Rest—I made sure to go to bed at a reasonable time and get at least nine hours of sleep a night.

What I learned:

Detox is hard! During a detox, the body is working extra hard to remove the offending toxins in the system, so you might not feel very good.

Your body needs healthy saturated fats to detox. The body needs to be nourished in order to detox, and this means plenty of animal fats.

Natural healing isn't a quick fix. It's a long process, but it is worth it in the end

Here's a chart of my blood levels over the past several years. Thyroperoxidase Ab and thyroglobulin are the two thyroid antibody levels that doctors use to diagnose a patient with Hashimoto's disease.

	TSH (.03-4.5) uIU/ml	Free T3 (2.0-4.4) pg/mL	Free T4 (.9-1.7) ng/dL	Thyroper-oxidase Ab (<=60)	Thyro-globulin Ab (<=60)
2/2010	58.34	5.6	0.4	>1300	211.2
7/2012	0.06	3.1	1.8	250	<20
Current	2.28	2.5	1.2	<60	<20

It took several years, but my blood levels eventually came back to normal. While everyone is different, I'm not alone in my healing of Hashimoto's. My nutritionist never claimed she could heal my disease, but she encouraged me to believe that the body is capable of tremendous regeneration, and so it was to that end we charged together. Kim taught me that healing comes through gentle, steady, and effective detoxification coupled with nutrient-dense, nourishing foods. It is my hope to shed light on what this looks like in a very attainable way.

If you're struggling with chronic health issues, I encourage you to seek out a nutritionist, osteopath, naturopath, or nutritional therapy practitioner who can help guide you toward better health. Even if everyone around you says it can't be done, follow your instincts. If you think it's possible, run toward that hope. After my experience, I truly believe that many of the diseases that ail us can be avoided or reversed with the right foods, detox, and support.

WHY GRAIN FREE INSTEAD OF GLUTEN FREE?

Many people ask why I went completely grain-free instead of only cutting out gluten. It can seem drastic, but when you realize how grains can affect a compromised immune system, eliminating them makes sense. When grains enter the body they cause the insulin levels in the blood to rise. When they are eaten in excess over time, the body becomes overtaxed, and eventually the excessive grains can cause inflammation in the body. Inflammation is the root cause of many health issues, including diabetes, allergies, arthritis, heart disease, tendinitis, and autoimmune diseases. A grain-free diet rich in nourishing foods gives the body time to rest, heal, and reduce inflammation.

Many who are diagnosed with food allergies or sensitivities think that if they just cut out the offending food, their problem is solved. For instance, someone with celiac disease will cut out gluten. But what many people misunderstand is that the root of their problem is inflammation. Removing all grains, instead of only those grains containing gluten, gives many people faster, more significant improvement in their health.

If you're ready to reduce inflammation, where should you begin? The best place to start is by eliminating all processed foods. Yes, all. Eat traditionally prepared, real food—foods free of pesticides, herbicides, and all chemicals are ideal. Animal foods derived from animals raised 100 percent on pasture or wild meats are anti-inflammatory. I know this may seem extreme, but to give the body time to rest and heal, it needs to be nourished with the right foods. I've walked down this path and, yes, it can be a pain at times, but after seeing how foods can heal, I would do it all again.

GRAINS TO AVOID

Avoid these grains when eating a grain-free diet:

Amaranth	Rice
Barley	Rye
Corn (including popcorn)	Sorghum
	Spelt
Farro	Teff
Fonio	
Kamut	Triticale
Millet	Wheat (including durum, semolina, bulgur)
Oats	
Quinoa	Wild rice

Though quinoa is technically a seed, many people have problems digesting quinoa because the body processes it more like a grain, so it's best to avoid it. It's important to remember that grains can lurk in unsuspecting places such as beverages, baking powder, and jarred and canned foods. Corn is an especially tricky ingredient, as it is found in almost every processed food on the shelf. That's another reason to cook and bake with unprocessed foods!

Here's a handy list of common additives and ingredients that may contain grain:

Ingredients

Acetic acid	Hydrolyzed vegetable protein
Alcohol	Iodized salt
Alpha tocopherol	Lactate
Artificial sweeteners	Lactic acid
Ascorbic acid	Lecithin
Aspartame	Magnesium citrate
Calcium citrate	Malic acid
Calcium lactate	Maltodextrin
Caramel and caramel color	Maltose
Cellulose	Modified food starch
Citric acid	MSG
Dextrose	Natural flavorings
Erythritol	Polysorbates
Ethanol	Saccharin
Ethylene	Sodium citrate
Ethyl acetate	Sorbic acid
Fruit juice concentrate	Sorbitol
Gluconic acid	Tocopherol
Glucose syrup	Vegetable starch
	Vitamin C

Foods

Baking powder	Distilled white vinegar
Confectioner's sugar	Commercial stevia
Corn oil	Yeast
Corn syrup	

MY PANTRY AND FRIDGE

If you're like most people, the thought of cooking without grains seems impossible at first. *No bread? No rice? No pasta? What's left?* The truth is you can still have grain-free versions of these foods if you want. But once you learn to look beyond the typical American dinner plate, you'll be amazed at the delicious variety of foods available to you. And you're likely to feel so great eating grain free, you won't miss a thing.

I want to walk you through the aisles of your local health food store—and in some cases, Internet sites—to introduce you to the ingredients I reach for most often when I'm cooking and baking. I like to stick with ingredients that can easily be found at my local store, but I've found that sometimes it's more economical to order online. (Check out the Resources section on page 283 for all of my favorite ways to make grain-free shopping as inexpensive as possible.)

Not everyone will decide to eat a 100 percent grain-free diet. Some people, depending on food sensitivities and health goals, will need to cut all traces of grain from their diets. Others will find vastly improved health by cutting out the most obvious sources of grains, such as wheat, corn, and rice. Experiment with your diet and pay close attention to how your body reacts to different ingredients in your food so that you can find what works best for you. If you decide to keep some grains in your diet, it's important that you understand how to properly prepare them so that they're digestible. This requires soaking the grains. Traditionally, grains were consumed whole after being soaked or fermented. Modern science has discovered the importance of this ancient practice. All grains contain phytic acid (an organic acid in which phosphorus is bound). Unreleased phytic acid binds to certain minerals, such as calcium, copper, iron, magnesium, and zinc, preventing their absorption in the intestinal tract. Over time, this can lead to conditions such as irritable bowel and leaky gut syndromes, and eventually much more serious disorders. Soaking grains in warm water combined with an acid such as yogurt, lemon juice, raw apple cider vinegar, or homemade whey allows the enzymes and probiotic organisms to break down and neutralize the phytic acid.

For the purposes of this book, we'll stick with a grain-free diet. This chapter gives you all the information you need to get your pantry and refrigerator stocked and ready for grain-free cooking and baking.

Grain-Free Flours

Flour is the ingredient that stumps beginners the most when they first consider avoiding grains in their diet. Think about flour and suddenly it's everywhere, in almost every prepared food that comes to mind. But don't worry! The gluten-free food market has exploded in recent years and substitutes for grains are easier to find than ever.

Almond Flour

Almond flour is made from pulverized almonds. I prefer to use blanched almond flour because the skins of the almonds, which contain phytic acid, have been removed. Phytic acid is an enzyme inhibitor—a substance that makes it difficult for your body to absorb nutrients. Almonds are high in omega-6 fatty acids, a beneficial fat, but one that's best to eat in moderation. Almond flour is very different from regular flours because it doesn't contain any gluten, so it works best when combined with other ingredients such as coconut flour or eggs, which will help the baked goods remain intact. It's a great flour to use for cakes, cookies, and muffins and for coating meats. I generally use a combination of 1 cup almond flour and a few tablespoons of coconut flour to substitute for 1 cup of white flour in a recipe.

Coconut Flour

Coconut flour is made from dried and powdered coconut meat. Coconut flour soaks up an incredible amount of moisture (which is why most recipes call for large quantities of eggs) and can lead to a very doughy and dense baked good if it isn't used carefully. While it's a bit more expensive than other ingredients, you don't need much in each recipe—a little goes a long way. Alone, it has a faint coconut taste, but when combined with other ingredients, the flavor is undetectable. I like to use it in baked goods because it gives them more structure. Coconut flour can be a bit tricky, so I suggest first trying recipes from this book to become familiar with how to use it.

Arrowroot Flour

Arrowroot flour is made from the bulb of the arrowroot plant, which is dried and ground into a powder. Arrowroot makes a perfect stand-in for cornstarch and can be substituted 1:1. I use it in baked goods when I'm looking for a more flaky consistency.

Tapioca Flour

Tapioca flour is extracted from the cassava root (a woody shrub native to South America) and it is great for thickening sauces. It acts very much like arrowroot, but is sometimes easier to find at the grocery store. It doesn't contain many nutrients and is higher in carbohydrates, so it's best to use it sparingly.

Bean Flours

Bean flours are made from dried and ground beans. They can be used as a thickener in soups and stews or as a flour to dredge meat in before sautéing. It's best to purchase sprouted bean flours to ensure proper digestion (see Resources, page 203). I use bean flours sparingly since they are higher in carbohydrates, but they're a nice alternative to nut flours.

Natural Sweeteners

While too much of any sweetener can contribute to inflammation, sometimes we want to add a little sweetness when baking or cooking. I prefer to stick with sweeteners as close to their original form as possible.

Raw Honey

Raw honey is a good choice for a sweetener because it contains beneficial enzymes that are lost during the processing and filtering of regular honey. I prefer to use a lighter honey, such as clover, because of its subtle flavor.

Maple Syrup

Maple syrup is rich in trace minerals and is a great choice for drizzling or for adding to chocolate recipes. I prefer Grade B because it's more economical and also contains more nutrients than Grade A. Grade B is a bit darker and has a more robust flavor than Grade A.

Maple Sugar

Maple sugar is made by dehydrating maple syrup. It's a bit more expensive than maple syrup but is a great substitute for white sugar.

Organic Whole Cane Sugar (Sucanat)

Organic whole cane sugar, or Sucanat, is made from dehydrated cane juice. It has a rich molasses flavor, so I enjoy using it in gingerbreads and spicier baked goods. Some brands are processed in factories with wheat, so be sure to read the label before purchasing if you have a wheat allergy.

Stevia

Stevia has gained much popularity in the past few years because of its super-sweet qualities and low carbohydrate content. It's five hundred times sweeter than regular sugar, so you need to add only a small amount. When shopping for stevia, it's best to look for a brand that is unprocessed. Stevia leaves are green, so if the stevia you find isn't green, it has probably gone through some processing and bleaching before hitting the shelves. Stevia can be easily grown at home. To use fresh stevia in cooking and baking, you simply cut the leaves off the stem, let them dehydrate for a few days at room temperature, and then crush them into a powder. The dried, crushed leaves should be stored in an airtight container and will last for about six months at room temperature.

Coconut Sugar/Palm Sugar

Coconut sugar is a traditional sugar made from the sap of coconut flowers. It's boiled down to create dry sugar blocks, a soft paste, or granules. I prefer it to white sugar in baking recipes.

Date Sugar

Date sugar is 100 percent dehydrated dates ground into small pieces. Date sugar doesn't dissolve in liquids, so it's better utilized for baked goods.

Sweeteners to Avoid

Agave

Agave was the beauty queen of alternative sweeteners for many years, but the truth behind this sweetener has come to light. Nutritionally, agave is similar to high-fructose corn syrup, as it can be as high as 90 percent concentrated fructose. Most labels say "raw," but for agave to have its famous delicate sweet taste, it has to be cooked. Recently the American Diabetes Association listed agave as a sweetener to be limited, and the Glycemic Index Institute removed agave from its list of "safe" sweeteners back in 2011.[*]

---

* http://webmd.com/diet/features/the-truth-about-agave

White Sugar, Raw Sugar, Turbinado, Brown Sugar

White sugar, raw sugar, turbinado, brown sugar, and any other chemically made and refined sweeteners should be avoided if improving or maintaining your health is a priority. While we should limit all sweeteners, it's best to stay away from sugars that have been bleached and chemically altered, and thus made devoid of nutrients.

Oils and Fats

Organic, Pastured Butter

Organic, pastured butter is made from the milk of cows that are raised under organic standards and are allowed to graze on pasture. Grass-fed butter contains higher amounts of omega-3 fatty acids than its conventional counterparts. And what about the idea that "fat makes you fat"? Well, butter is a short-chain fatty acid that's used quickly for energy and is rarely stored as fat. Butter is also an excellent source of cholesterol, which the body uses to make hormones. The fatty acids found in butter have antimicrobial properties that can help protect the body from viruses and pathogenic bacteria.

Virgin Coconut Oil

Virgin coconut oil is a medium-chain fatty acid that is great for low- to medium-temperature cooking. It's a rich, saturated fat that has antimicrobial as well as antiviral properties. I prefer to use this oil in baked goods, desserts, and Asian cooking.

Olive Oil

Olive oil is most beneficial when used in its raw form or processed at medium to low heat. Olive oil has a medium smoke point (when it visually starts to smoke), so it's best for cooking at a medium heat or lower to prevent oxidation, which breaks down the nutrients. Look for olive oil that is extra virgin, cold-pressed, and unfiltered. Since the standards here in America are very loose for olive oil labeling, it's best to call the company and ask how the oil is processed. My favorite brands of olive oil are listed in the Resources section on page 283.

Lard and Tallow

Lard and tallow—rendered fat from pigs and cows—have really gotten a bad rap the last few decades. Lard and tallow used to be the first choice of housewives until Crisco and vegetable oil came along. Grass-fed lard and tallow are rich in CLA (conjugated linoleic acid), a strong anti-inflammatory, and have omega 6:3 ratios similar to many fatty fish. They are great fats to use for the occasional frying recipe. When shopping for lard and tallow, look for brands that haven't been bleached, deodorized, hydrogenated, or altered in any way. Check the Resources section on page 283 for my favorite sources.

Ghee

Ghee, or clarified butter, has become one of my favorite cooking fats. It can withstand high temperatures without oxidizing or smoking and lends a nice buttery, nutty flavor. Many who are lactose intolerant can handle ghee because it's pure butter oil, with the milk solids removed. Also, if you make it from organic, pastured butter, it contains many nutrients (higher amounts of omega-3 fatty acids and conjugated linoleic acid). It's very easy to make; simply melt butter and then skim off the milk solids. I usually make a batch over the weekend, store it in a Mason jar, and then use the ghee throughout the week (see page 255 for a recipe). It's great for sautéing at high heats, roasting, and pan frying.

Duck Fat

Duck fat is highly prized in Europe and quite a treat to use. As with fat from other animals, the nutrients will depend on the duck's diet, so it's best to find fat from a duck that was raised outdoors on a natural diet.

Flaxseed Oil

Flaxseed oil is rich in omega-3 fatty acids and is best used cold. It has a smoke point of only 250°F, so steer clear of this oil in any baking or cooking as the oil will oxidize. It's a great oil to drizzle over salads, add to a morning smoothie, or use over other cold dishes. It's best to use flaxseed oil in small quantities because the body absorbs it slowly.

Palm Shortening

Palm shortening, also known as clarified palm oil, is a nice dairy-free fat to use in baking and cooking. It does not contain any trans fats and has a neutral flavor. Some companies support deforestation in order to produce palm oils, so it's important to buy from a reliable, sustainable source (see Resources, page 283).

Oils and Fats to Avoid

Many of the oils used in the modern American diet are hazardous to our health. They are processed, cleaned with chemicals, and often come from genetically modified corn or soy. Most oils found in the grocery store aisles are heated to very high tempera-tures during processing; this heat oxidizes the oils. Oxidation creates free radicals that can damage our cells. The processing increases the shelf life of the oils and removes most of the natural flavoring, making them more attractive for the food industry but less healthy for the consumer. Vegetable oils, such as canola, corn, and soy oil, are usually made from genetically modified crops. So, I suggest you limit the use of such oils and stick with unrefined oils and fats.

Other Essentials for Your Pantry and Fridge

Coconut Milk

Coconut milk is a prized dairy alternative and offers many beneficial nutrients. I try to use coconut milk that contains few preservatives, so I prefer brands that come in a BPA-free can or make it myself. Do not confuse coconut milk with the coconut milk beverage that's found in the refrigerated section of the grocery store. Most coconut beverages contain preservatives and additives and are closer to soft drinks than milk. Coconut milk is a great replacement for heavy cream, and you can even make buttermilk and dairy-free sour cream by adding some lemon juice to the milk and letting it ferment.

Raw Milk and Cream

Raw—unpasteurized and nonhomogenized—milk and cream are nourishing foods if your body can tolerate dairy. (Check www.RealMilk.com for sources in your area.) Pasteurization is a process of heating milk to kill bacteria. Unfortunately, this process also typically destroys friendly bacteria (probiotics) and vitamins, including vitamin A, and more than 30 percent of the vitamin B complex. When probiotic bacteria are destroyed, the milk becomes more vulnerable to contamination. After pasteurization, vitamins that were destroyed are often replaced with synthetic vitamins. One percent and 2 percent milk sold in stores may contain nonfat dried milk, which is oxidized and therefore may contain oxidized cholesterol, which studies suggest may promote heart disease.

Homogenization is a process that takes place after pasteurization. In one method, for example, milk is pushed through small tapered tubes under high pressure to break apart the fat molecules. This is why homogenized milk doesn't have to be shaken—the cream doesn't rise to the top. Unfortunately, the structure of the fat molecules actually changes during this process. Not only are the new fat molecules difficult to digest, they have also been linked to heart disease.[*]

Unpasteurized milk from grass-fed cows is full of nutrients and probiotics such as *Lactobacillus acidophilus*, B6, B12, vitamins A and D, and calcium, and it's rich in CLAs (conjugated linoleic acids). In other words, unpasteurized milk promotes good bacteria, sound digestion, and a healthy cardiovascular system.

Celtic Sea Salt

Salt may seem like an insignificant topic, but if you want to take steps toward a less processed diet, it's something to think about. Basic table salt is first pro-

Celtic sea salt

cessed at high temperatures, removing vital minerals from the salt; it's then iodized, bleached, and mixed with anticaking agents (examples include ferrocyanide, yellow prussiate of soda, tricalcium phosphate, aluminum-calcium silicate, and sodium aluminosilicate). Iodine is a vital mineral that supports thyroid function, body metabolism, and reproductive tissue health, among other benefits. The Dietary Reference Intake (DRI) is set at 150–1,100 mcg a day. But the amount of iodine in a moderate serving of iodized salt is 1,520 mcg, so it is easy to exceed the daily limit using even a modest amount of salt.

On the other hand, a quality, gently processed sea salt can offer myriad beneficial trace minerals. The only brand I've found that fits the bill is Celtic sea salt. It's hand-harvested off the coast of France, dried at low temperatures, and contains no additives, bleaching agents, or anti-caking agents. Celtic sea salt provides more than eighty trace minerals (including iodine) and helps balance electrolyte and alkaline/acid levels.

* J. P. Zikakis, S. J. Rzuidlo, and N. O. Biasoto, "Persistence of bovine milk xanthine oxidase activity after gastric digestion in vivo and in vitro," *Journal of Dairy Science* 60, no. 4 (April 1977): 533; K. Oster, "Plasmalogen diseases: a new concept of the etiology of the atherosclerotic process," *American Journal of Clinical Research* 2 (1971): 30–35.

I prefer cooking with Celtic sea salt not only for its health benefits but also because of its flavor. The grains bring a subtle saltiness and complement foods better than any other salt I've tried. If you can't find Celtic sea salt, try to find an unprocessed salt that is free of preservatives and anticaking agents.

Fermented Tamari Sauce

Also known as Nama shoyu, this makes for a great grain-free substitution for soy sauce. When properly fermented and raw, tamari contains probiotics that are beneficial for the gut. A few companies, such as Ohsawa, make tamari the old-fashioned way, brewed in wooden kegs and allowed to age and ferment.

Herbamare and Other Preservative-Free Seasoning Mixes

I prefer to use organic, nonirradiated spices and herbs in my cooking. Irradiation—a process through which ionizing radiation in the form of gamma rays, x-rays, or electrons generated from machines are used to kill bacteria in food—is performed on almost all nonorganic spices, so I opt for the natural alternative. Herbamare is one of my favorite organic seasoning blends to season poultry, beef, fish, and vegetables. Check out the Resources section on page 283.

Homemade Baking Powder

Many baking powders contain not only aluminum but also cornstarch, which derives from grain. Mixing your own baking powder takes only a few minutes and is another easy way to eliminate processed ingredients from your diet (see page 272).

Almond and Vanilla Extracts

Almond and vanilla extracts are great to have on hand to take your baked goods to the next level, and vanilla extract can even be made at home (see page 274). For the extracts I can't make myself, I buy an organic version that is free of extra preservatives or sweeteners.

Eggs

Eggs from pastured chickens are higher in omega-3 fatty acids and vitamin E,[*] so be sure to look for "pastured" or "pasture-raised" on the label.

Grass-Fed Gelatin

Gelatin is my favorite binding agent to use in grain-free baked goods. It's flavorless, so it can be used in any type of dish. It contains six to twelve grams of protein per tablespoon, helps aid in digestion, and can benefit the immune system, heart, muscles, and skin. Not all gelatin is created equal, so it's important to purchase from a good source. Bernard Jensen and Great Lakes gelatins both come from grass-fed animals and don't contain MSG (most other brands of gelatin do contain MSG).

Fermented Foods

Fermented foods such as sauerkraut, kombucha, kefir, and relishes are a great addition to the diet. Fermented foods contain millions of good bacteria (also known as probiotics) and thus help aid in digestion and keep our gut and immune systems healthy. The

---

[*] C. J. Lopez-Bote et al., "Effect of free-range feeding on omega-3 fatty acids and alpha-tocopherol content and oxidative stability of eggs," *Animal Feed Science and Technology* 72 (1998): 33–40.

lactobacilli in fermented vegetables contain helpful enzymes as well as antibiotic and anticarcinogenic substances and promote healthy flora throughout the intestine. Fermenting is usually as simple as chopping up vegetables, adding Celtic sea salt, putting them in a jar, and letting them sit at room temperature for a few days (see pages 258–61). For further reading, I recommend the book *Wild Fermentation: The Flavor, Nutrition, and Craft of Live-Culture Foods* by Sandor Ellix Katz.

Meats, Poultry, and Seafood

Organic, Grass-Fed Beef

Organic, grass-fed beef has two to four times more omega-3 fatty acids than meat from grain-fed animals. Grass-fed animals also contain less fat in their meat and more vitamin A, vitamin E, antioxidants, and linoleic acid. Organic beef hasn't been treated with synthetic hormones or antibiotics, and the feed the cattle eat is also organic. Since grass-fed beef can be costly, I prefer to buy directly from the farm, where I can save hundreds of dollars each year.[*]

Chicken

Chicken's popularity has made raising it a more and more industrial process, so it's best to buy chicken that is raised on a pasture and is fed organic, non-GMO feed. Pasture-raised, organic chicken is higher in omega-3 fatty acids, and the meat won't contain any of the antibiotics that are usually administered to conventionally raised poultry.

Fish and Shrimp

Fish and shrimp raised on farms are often fed fish meal that contains ingredients such as animal by-products and by-products from the milling and food processing industries. The fish are also occasionally given additives that color their flesh. When shopping for fish, look for fresh fish that has been caught in the wild and is free of preservatives.

Lamb

Lamb raised on a pasture has been found to be higher in protein and lower in fat than conventionally raised lamb.[†]

Pork

Pork that is raised on pasture without growth hormones or antibiotics can be beneficial to the body. I prefer to purchase pork, such as bacon and ham, that has no added sugars or nitrates.

Game

Game meats such as deer, quail, and elk contain many nutrients and good fats because they have been able to grow and roam in the wild, as nature intended.

WHAT ABOUT SATURATED FATS?

We've all heard the claims that saturated fats and cholesterol cause heart disease. We've practically been raised on the idea. But you might be surprised—as I was—to find that the "scientific" evidence isn't very scientific.

---

[*] Cynthia A. Daley et al., "A review of fatty acid profiles and antioxidant content in grass-fed and grain-fed beef," *Nutrition Journal* 9 (2010): 10.

[†] http://www.spcru.ars.usda.gov/research/publications/publications .htm?SEQ_NO_115=73942

The low-fat message began in the 1950s with a theory called the "lipid hypothesis." This theory proposes a direct relationship between the amount of saturated fat and cholesterol in the diet and the incidence of coronary heart disease. Ancel Keys, the researcher behind the lipid hypothesis, received a lot of publicity, especially from the vegetable oil and food processing industries. Many experts still preach the benefits of a diet low in fat and cholesterol for decreasing the risk of heart disease, but I was shocked to learn there is very little scientific evidence to support this claim.

As Sally Fallon and Mary G. Enig, PhD, write in their book *Nourishing Traditions*,

> Today heart disease causes at least 40 percent of all US deaths. If, as we have been told, heart disease results from the consumption of saturated fats, one would expect to find a corresponding increase in animal fat in the American diet. Actually, the reverse is true. During the sixty-year period from 1910 to 1970, the proportion of traditional animal fat in the American diet declined from 83 percent to 62 percent, and butter consumption plummeted from 18 pounds per person per year to four. During the past eighty years, dietary cholesterol intake has increased only 1 percent. During the same period the percentage of dietary vegetable oils in the form of margarine, shortening and refined oils increased about 400 percent while the consumption of sugar and processed foods increased about 60 percent.

Multiple studies and research from reputable doctors and scientists suggest fat and cholesterol may not be the enemies we've made them out to be. A study published in the American Society for Nutrition determined that "there is no significant evidence for concluding that dietary saturated fat is associated with an increased risk of CHD or CVD."[*]

Another study published by the National Institutes of Health followed 1,782 men for more than twelve years and concluded: "A high intake of dairy fat was associated with a lower risk of central obesity and a low dairy fat intake was associated with a higher risk of central obesity."[†] Wow! This is just the tip of the iceberg. More studies have surfaced over the years proving that saturated fat and cholesterol aren't the villains we thought they were.

I'm not a scientist or doctor, but here's what I've learned:

1. **A fat like butter** is a short fatty-acid chain that is quickly absorbed into the body for energy and plays a vital role in the immune system.

2. **Coconut oil**, a medium fatty-acid chain, has high antimicrobial properties. It's also used quickly for energy and contributes to the health of the immune system.

3. **Olive oil** is a long fatty-acid chain and supports many processes at the cellular level.

4. **Polyunsaturated fats**, such as corn, safflower, canola, and soy, are needed in very small quantities,

---

[*] P. W. Siri-Tarino, Q. Sun, F. B. Hu, and R. M. Karuss, "Meta-analysis of prospective cohort studies evaluating the association of saturated fat with cardiovascular disease," *American Journal of Clinical Nutrition* 91 (2010): 535–546.

[†] Sara Holmberg and Anders Thelin, "High dairy fat intake related to less central obesity: A male cohort study with 12 years' follow-up," *Scandinavian Journal of Primary Health Care* 31, no. 2 (June 2013): 89–94.

but unfortunately we consume them in mass quantities from processed sources. High levels of polyunsaturated fats have been shown to contribute to many diseases, including cancer, heart disease, digestive disorders, and weight gain.

5. We consume too many omega-6 fats (mainly from commercially processed vegetable oils) and not enough omega-3s (from pastured eggs, meats, dairy, and fish). Omega-6 fatty acids can contribute to heart disease, weight gain, and inflammation in the body. Omega-3 fatty acids decrease inflammation and strengthen the immune system. My nutritionist, Kim Schuette at Biodynamic Wellness, says that the ratio of our omega-3 to omega-6 intake should be between 2:1 and 1:1 to maintain a healthy immune system and reduce inflammation. This balanced ratio is in line with that of our ancestors. Today, the estimated ratio range for many individuals averages 10:1 to 20:1 and some average up to 25:1.

6. Saturated fats are needed for healthy bones, to protect the liver from toxins, and to enhance the immune system, among other purposes.

7. Saturated fatty acids give our cells necessary stiffness and integrity.

8. When our arteries "clog up," only about one quarter of the fat found inside is saturated fat. So much for that myth! The other three-quarters is unsaturated fat, and most of that is *poly*unsaturated.* As we know, processed foods are the biggest culprits when it comes to polyunsaturated fats.

---

* C. V. Felton et al., "Dietary polyunsaturated fatty acids and composition of human aortic plaques," *Lancet* 344, no. 8931 (October 1994): 1195.

Almost ten years ago, after a year or two of my own reading and research, I decided the evidence was compelling enough to give fats a try. I got rid of all the processed fats and oils in my pantry (vegetable oil, canola oil, corn oil, and so on) and replaced them with butter, coconut oil, olive oil, and a few others. The result? I felt better and my energy level improved. Getting sick is a rarity in our family these days.

If you're reading this information for the first time, I know it can be confusing and a bit overwhelming. I understand—I felt the same way. Remember, it's all about little changes. Take some time, read and research for yourself, and see what you decide. I think you'll be amazed at what you find.

EQUIPMENT

A sharp knife, a heavy 12-inch skillet, and tongs are my all-time favorite pieces of equipment in the kitchen. With just these three things, I can do quite a bit of cooking. In general, I like to keep things basic with my equipment, but sometimes I'll buy something fun—such as an ice cream maker—if I know I'll use it often.

A Few Basics

Here are some of my favorite pieces of equipment for cooking and baking. I like to "buy for life" if I can afford it. For instance, if I'm going to buy a knife, I wait until I can afford a good one that will last a lifetime.

Sharp Knives

A dull knife is actually more dangerous than a sharp one, so it's very important to keep your knives sharp. I don't think it's necessary to buy a sixteen-piece knife set to be successful in the kitchen. My essentials are an 8-inch chef's knife, a paring knife, and a serrated bread knife. I prefer brands such as Henckels or Wusthof because they are sturdy and made of high-carbon steel, which resists stains and corrosion.

Cutting Board

Choose a cutting board that doesn't slide around and is large enough to cut a few onions on at a time. I do have a wooden board, but I prefer to use my thick polyethylene boards because they are pretty much indestructible and are also dishwasher safe. My favorite size is 11 x 17 inches.

Food Processor

A food processor comes in handy when making things like piecrusts and pesto, or when you need to chop vegetables quickly. This was the first piece of equipment I purchased when we set up our kitchen many years ago. From grating and slicing to processing, this little machine saves me lots of time in the kitchen. A 10-cup or 14-cup Cuisinart or Kitchen-Aid food processor is a good choice.

Standing Mixer

While not a necessity, a standing mixer is a beloved tool in the kitchen. It will save time and energy when whipping up some cream or creaming butter and sugar. And with all of the lovely colors available now, it will add a bit of sparkle to your work area. I prefer the classic KitchenAid mixer.

Spice Grinder

A $20 coffee grinder will grind fresh spices to just the right consistency. If you also use it for coffee, just remember to wipe it out well. No one likes cumin-spiced coffee or coffee-flavored cumin!

Whisk

A 10-inch balloon whisk is a great tool for both cooking and baking. I prefer a whisk made of stainless steel. It's sturdy and dishwasher safe.

Heat-Proof Spatula

A few good spatulas are a necessity in the kitchen. You can use them on the stove when sautéing or to scrape the last bits of batter out of the mixing bowl. They come in fun colors, too.

Mixing Bowls

Mixing bowls are essential for baking. I also use mine for tossing salads. There's no need to buy fancy, expensive mixing bowls. Simple glass Pyrex bowls are sturdy, dishwasher safe, and available in all sizes. You can purchase them in sets or individually. I have two 4-quart mixing bowls I use for everything.

Measuring Cups

Did you know there is a difference between dry and liquid measuring cups? Liquids should be measured in liquid measuring cups and dry ingredients such as flour and sugar in dry measuring cups. This can make a significant difference in your baking, so it's a good idea to have both kinds. A good ol' Pyrex liquid measuring cup is cheap and will last for years. I've used many different dry measuring cups, and one of my favorites is the KitchenArt adjustable half-cup scoop. It's compact and easy to use.

> If you're looking for good equipment but don't know which brand to purchase, check out the reviews by *Cook's Illustrated* magazine. They do blind tests, don't allow any advertising, and are completely unbiased. Whenever I need a piece of kitchen equipment, I check out their advice, and they've never steered me wrong! Their reviews and recipes now require a paid membership, but over the past sixteen years that I've been a subscriber, I've found it worth every penny.

Stainless Steel Colander

A stainless steel colander costs about $20 and is pretty much indestructible. It's useful for washing lettuces and fruits.

Glass Jars

I prefer jars for storing nuts, seeds, sweeteners, and so on in my pantry. The jars are clear, so there's no need to label, and the glass prevents the food from absorbing odors. Sturdy large glass jars can be found at cookware stores. I prefer Mason jars or Bormioli Rocco Fido canning jars. I also reuse pickle, jam, and mustard jars to store small amounts of foods. It's an economical way to collect jars.

Blender

I know there are $600 blenders out there that can puree just about anything, but I like to keep it simple. A blender that has a good motor and large glass jar is a great piece of equipment—I use mine at least once a day to blend smoothies or salad dressing.

Candy Thermometer

For ultimate precision, a candy thermometer is perfect for candy, jelly, and deep-frying. I use a simple $10 candy thermometer and it works nicely.

Tongs

Tongs are a valuable kitchen tool and are like an extension of your hand. I use them to flip chicken in a skillet, toss salads, grill, and turn vegetables when roasting. I have at least five pairs of these in my kitchen. I prefer the 12-inch OXO Good Grips locking tongs.

Cookware and Bakeware

We spend a lot of time thinking about the foods we eat, but sometimes overlook the importance of the cookware we use to prepare them. It's important to use cookware without coatings or substances that can leach into our food. Studies have found that nonstick and aluminum cookware—two of the most popular types—tend to leach metals and other harmful chemicals into the food.

Stainless Steel Baking Sheets and Muffin Pans

Most bakeware sold in stores is made of an aluminum alloy. This aluminum can leach into our food. Nonstick and silicone-coated pans can also leach harmful chemicals and gases into food and into the air, so I stick with stainless steel, ceramic, stone, and glass. Stainless steel is a great choice for an all-purpose baking sheet. It heats evenly and is very sturdy. They are a bit more expensive than aluminum, but these pans last a lifetime.

Loaf Pans and Pie Plates

America's Test Kitchen taught me many years ago that glass loaf pans and pie plates are one of the best choices for baking pies and quick breads. They heat evenly and are affordable. I have two Pyrex loaf pans and two Pyrex 9-inch pie plates for baking.

Baking Dishes

Ceramic and glass baking dishes are my favorites. When I make a casserole or roast meats, I like a good, sturdy dish that heats evenly. I have 8 x 8-inch, 13 x 9-inch, and 11 x 7-inch baking dishes. These are three sizes commonly called for in recipes. Pyrex glass dishes are a great option.

Ramekins

These little ceramic bowls aren't a necessity, but I've found them very useful when making custards, individual pot pies, and puddings. I prefer the 6-ounce size because it's more standard than the 4-ounce bowls. I also keep one on the counter next to the stove and fill it with Celtic sea salt so it's handy for cooking and baking.

Stainless Steel Pots and Pans

Stainless steel is one of my favorite types of cookware. It's a nonreactive metal that doesn't corrode or pit like other materials can. It's durable enough to last a lifetime. Almost all of my pots and pans are stainless steel. I've had them for more than ten years and they're still beautiful! I found a few articles that said stainless steel could release very small amounts of nickel into the food, but I had a hard time finding anything conclusive. If you're sensitive to nickel, you might want to avoid stainless steel and choose enameled cookware. The key to keeping foods from sticking is the heat level. I cook sunny-side-up eggs in ghee in my stainless steel skillet over medium-high heat. It really works!

Ceramic/Enamel Cookware

This is a great option for those who love the even heating of cast iron but don't want to bother with the seasoning process. The cast iron is coated in a hard enamel, making it somewhat nonstick and very easy to clean. Le Creuset has some beautiful, colorful enamel pieces.

Cast Iron Cookware

Cast iron cookware is a great conductor of heat and is very economical. Acids can cause some iron leaching, so it's best to avoid cooking acidic foods (such as tomatoes) in cast iron. I prefer to buy untreated cast iron, as most preseasoned pans have been seasoned with soy oil. Look online for tutorials on seasoning and cleaning your cast iron pans.

These are the sizes of pots and pans I use most often:

12-inch stainless steel skillet

3-quart stainless steel saucepan with lid

Dutch oven (a large, oven-safe pot with a lid)—
    I use the 8-quart size

6-inch stainless steel skillet—great for cooking up
    small batches of scrambled eggs

1-quart stainless steel saucepan—I actually own two
    of these because I use them all the time!

Nonessentials, but Fun to Have

Ice Cream Maker

A 1-quart ice cream maker costs about $50 and is an extremely fun tool. Frozen yogurts, sorbets, ice cream—you can make them all in your own kitchen without any chemical additives or preservatives. I keep the bowl in the freezer, so when we get an ice cream craving, we're ready to whip some up at home.

Immersion Blender

I have a $20 immersion blender that has served me well for many years. It comes in handy when I need to puree soups or make a quick salad dressing and I would rather not pull out the countertop blender. It's a great tool for the kids to use because it's small and easy to handle.

Juicer

It's very difficult to find fresh, organic juice in stores, so if you enjoy drinking unpasteurized juice, then a juicer is a great piece of equipment to own. I prefer a juicer that doesn't use much heat to extract the juice so that fewer nutrients are lost. The Bella NutriPro and Green Star are good choices.

Spiralizer

This little gadget turns ordinary vegetables into noodles. When you're on a grain-free diet, it's worth the $30 splurge to be able to twirl and twist "noodles" onto your fork. You can "noodle" all sorts of squash and root vegetables to create quick weeknight dinners.

HOW TO ADAPT RECIPES

Do you have cookbooks and food magazines that you love and still want to use? Most recipes can be easily adapted to be grain free, so you can still use most of your favorite recipes with just a few tweaks. While substitutions for cooking are usually pretty easy, baking recipes can be a bit more tricky. I suggest trying some of the recipes in this book first before branching out on your own so you can understand how the ingredients look, feel, and handle.

My preference is to use raw honey or maple syrup as a substitute for white sugar. But while this will work in many recipes, success is not guaranteed. In developing and testing recipes for this book, I found that using honey in the piecrust and pancake recipes caused those foods to darken and burn very quickly; if I used maple or coconut sugar instead, I didn't have that problem. So as you go along, if you find that baked goods made with honey are browning too quickly, substitute a granulated sweetener such as coconut sugar or Sucanat.

To show you how I transform recipes from traditional to grain free, here's an example of a recipe that I converted. It's my recipe for Blackberry Apple Crisp from my first cookbook, *Deliciously Organic*, which I adapted from whole wheat to grain free.

Blackberry Apple Crisp

Original Whole Wheat Version

FILLING

3 apples, preferably Gala, peeled and cut into large bite-size pieces

2 cups blackberries, fresh or frozen

Grated zest of 1 lemon

Grated zest of 1 orange

2 tablespoons lemon juice

2 tablespoons orange juice

2 tablespoons whole wheat pastry flour

⅓ cup whole cane sugar or Sucanat

½ teaspoon ground cinnamon

TOPPING

1 cup whole wheat pastry flour

¾ cup whole cane sugar or Sucanat

2 tablespoons maple syrup

¼ teaspoon sea salt

8 tablespoons (1 stick) unsalted butter, cut into 8 pieces

½ cup rolled oats

½ cup heavy cream (optional)

Blackberry Apple Crisp

Grain-Free Adaptation

FILLING

3 apples, preferably Gala, peeled and cut into large bite-size pieces

2 cups blackberries, fresh or frozen

Grated zest of 1 lemon

Grated zest of 1 orange

2 tablespoons lemon juice

2 tablespoons orange juice

1 tablespoon arrowroot flour (*The flour in the original filling is used as a thickener. Arrowroot is the perfect substitution, but I reduced it by half.*)

¼ cup coconut sugar (*I reduced the sugar by a few tablespoons and replaced it with coconut sugar since coconut sugar has a lower glycemic index.*)

½ teaspoon ground cinnamon

TOPPING

1 cup almond flour (*I use my combination of almond flour, coconut flour, and gelatin as a replacement for the 1 cup whole wheat flour.*)

2 tablespoons coconut flour

½ teaspoon unflavored grass-fed gelatin

½ cup coconut sugar (*I reduced the sugar by ¼ cup and replaced it with coconut sugar since coconut sugar has a lower glycemic index.*)

1 tablespoon raw honey

¼ teaspoon Celtic sea salt

8 tablespoons (1 stick) cold unsalted butter, cut into tablespoons

½ cup unsweetened coconut flakes (*These are a great substitute for oats in baked goods. You get a similar texture without the grain.*)

½ cup heavy cream (optional)

I followed the original recipe instructions and just swapped out the ingredients noted. See page 214 for the full recipe.

We can make noodles
out of anything!

Here's a handy substitution chart to help you convert your own favorite recipes to unprocessed and grain-free versions.

Instead of this	Use this	Substitution ratio
1 cup all-purpose flour	1 cup almond flour, 2 tablespoons coconut flour, and ½ teaspoon unflavored gelatin (this works for most baked goods such as cookies, cakes, and bars)	
Baking powder	Homemade Grain-Free Baking Powder (page 272)	1:1
1 cup whole wheat flour	¼ cup coconut flour (this won't work for all recipes, but is a good place to start)	
Cornstarch	Arrowroot or tapioca flour	1:1
Rice vinegar	Coconut vinegar	1:1
Cooked brown rice	"Riced" Cauliflower (page 263)	1:1
Pasta	Zucchini "noodles"	1:2
White sugar	Coconut sugar, maple sugar, or Sucanat (I always reduce the amount of sweetener by at least a quarter)	1:¾
	Honey or maple syrup (this substitution can be a bit more tricky, but generally I use half the amount of honey or maple syrup to replace white sugar)	1:½
Corn syrup	Maple syrup or honey heated to 220°F	1:1
1 cup brown sugar	¾ cup coconut sugar plus 1 tablespoon honey or maple syrup (combine until moist)	1:¾
One 14-ounce can sweetened condensed milk	2¼ cups coconut milk + ⅓ cup honey, cooked over low heat until reduced by half (for the full recipe, see page 275)	
Soy sauce	Coconut aminos or fermented tamari sauce	1:1

HOW TO EAT OUT

Eating out can be a challenge. Unfortunately, most chain restaurants put grains at the center of their menus or use unhealthy ingredients such as soy, trans fats, or processed vegetable oils. Restaurants that do use unprocessed, grain-free ingredients can be pricey. So since it's more expensive in general to eat out, our family goes out to eat only once every couple of months. I know this may sound drastic, but after you begin to realize how good you feel on an unprocessed, grain-free diet, it's easy to say "no" to the quick fast food.

Before going to a restaurant, I do my homework. I look for places that use local ingredients and I read over their menus online. If a restaurant uses fresh ingredients and has a good number of gluten-free options, I'll investigate it further. I also look for nonchain restaurants unless that chain is known for fresh, local, and gluten-free food.

When traveling I'll search online for organic restaurants or contact the Weston A. Price Foundation chapter leader or Slow Food International for the area, and will usually find a great place that serves fresh foods. There are also apps such as Locate Special Diet, Find Green, and Clean Plates that will help you locate healthy restaurants.

If I'm at a restaurant with friends and didn't have a say in picking the place, I usually stick with a protein and salad, and I always ask for olive oil and vinegar (don't just say "oil and vinegar" because they could bring you a vegetable oil). I also ask that my meat be grilled or broiled. I've learned that when I'm out for breakfast, if I ask kindly, the chef is more than willing to cook some eggs in butter or ghee instead of vegetable oil. The key is asking kindly!

HOW TO ENCOURAGE YOUR KIDS TO EAT GRAIN FREE

What if a grain-free diet is a new concept to your family? Is it even possible to change your children's diets without a struggle? It is! My kids were eight and ten when we started our grain-free journey, so they were used to eating lots of grains, but they transitioned to a grain-free diet with very little trouble.

My best advice, assuming you don't have a health issue that requires an immediate and thorough renovation of your diet, is to start slowly and introduce something new once a week. If your kids love pancakes, make a batch of grain-free pancakes. (For easy school-morning breakfasts you can make the pancakes ahead of time, then put them in the freezer and reheat a few at a time in the oven.) Instead of removing crackers and granola bars all at once, slowly start substituting vegetables, dips, raw cheeses, and meats. Invite some of their friends over and let the kids make homemade fruit snacks (see page 238) using molds in fun shapes.

When you do introduce new foods, I find it's best not to announce to the kids that something is different about their food that day. They might have preconceived ideas that could result in a negative response. When I introduced new foods, I served them as I would anything else, and then after the meal I asked the kids how they liked it. Ninety-nine percent of the time they had no idea I had changed anything.

Of course there are some days when the changes won't be welcomed. That's okay. When that happens, don't make a big deal of it. Just move on and try that food again somewhere down the road.

The idea is to ease the family into a healthier lifestyle without the disruption of a sudden, major shift in their diets. As their palates adjust to cleaner, more nutritious foods, they'll start to lose their taste for highly processed foods and will prefer these new recipes.

Breakfast

Breakfast is an important meal, and the typical American breakfast usually consists of sugars and carbohydrates. The problem with a grain and sugar breakfast is that it will leave you feeling depleted and hungry just a couple hours after eating, because your blood sugar levels will surge and then rapidly fall. Starting the day with healthy fats from organic butter, pastured eggs, or good bacon will satiate the body and give it the fuel it needs to work throughout the morning. In fact, our family has found that when we eat a nourishing breakfast, many times we aren't even hungry when lunchtime comes because our bodies have received enough nutrients and fats to keep us going for many hours.

While juicing is a popular way to get your nutrients at breakfast, it's important to remember that fruits and vegetables contain fat-soluble vitamins, which means they can only be absorbed when fat is present. Aside from being delicious, that pat of butter you sauté your eggs and kale in is key to making the vitamins in the kale available to your body. Egg yolks are often frowned upon, but they are a powerhouse of nutrients. Egg yolks from pastured chickens are rich in choline, cholesterol, and other brain-nourishing substances. I like to add raw yolks to smoothies in the mornings for added nutrition. (Don't worry, you can't taste them at all—in fact, they make the smoothie creamier!)

Our family prefers to cook eggs or blend a smoothie for breakfast. Both options are quick and the variations are endless. When we have a bit more time I love pulling out the waffle iron to make bacon and Cheddar waffles, or preparing a sausage strata for a holiday morning.

Grain-Free Biscuits

I'm from Texas, so I love a good biscuit with butter and jam on a slow Saturday morning. Give me a biscuit and a cup of coffee with raw heavy cream and I'm one happy girl. These biscuits are best eaten within a few hours after baking. They can also be frozen after baking, then reheated in a 300°F oven for about 10 minutes.

1. Preheat the oven to 350°F and adjust the rack to the middle position. Line a baking sheet with unbleached parchment paper.

2. Place the almond flour, coconut flour, salt, baking soda, and baking powder in the bowl of a food processor and pulse 2 or 3 times to combine. Cut the butter into chunks, add to the food processor, and pulse 8 to 10 times, until the mixture looks like wet sand with pea-size clumps of butter. Add the coconut milk and ¼ cup water and process until the mixture forms a dough. The mixture should be tacky but not loose or runny. If it's too loose, pulse in a tablespoon of almond flour.

3. Using a 2 inch cookie scoop, scoop mounds of dough and place them on the prepared baking sheet. Using your fingers, press gently on the tops of the dough mounds to flatten them just a little and give them a biscuit shape. Bake for 20 to 25 minutes, until golden brown on the edges.

PALEO/DAIRY-FREE ADAPTATION: Use ¼ cup of cold lard or tallow in place of the butter.

MAKES 1 DOZEN 3-INCH BISCUITS
PREPARATION TIME: 40 minutes

2½ cups almond flour, plus more as needed

1 tablespoon coconut flour

½ teaspoon Celtic sea salt

½ teaspoon baking soda

2 teaspoons Grain-Free Baking Powder (page 272)

5 tablespoons cold unsalted butter

¼ cup canned coconut milk

Quick Chia Seed Strawberry Jam

No hot jars or sticky mess! This jam is easy and quick to prepare and makes for a nice condiment on the breakfast table. Or put it in a cute jar and give it as a gift to a new neighbor.

Chia seeds are high in omega-3 fatty acids and contain alpha-linolenic acid (ALA) and linoleic acid (LA). They also contain protein, fiber, and some antioxidants. When mixed with the liquid from the strawberries, honey, and lemon juice, these exotic seeds turn very gelatinous, creating a quick and delicious jam.

Place the strawberries (with their juices) and honey in a large bowl. Using a muddler or the back of a fork, mash the strawberries and honey together until juices are released. Let the mixture sit at room temperature for 10 minutes to macerate. Stir in the chia seeds and lemon juice. Chill for at least 30 minutes before serving. Store the jam in an airtight container in the refrigerator. The jam will keep for about 10 days in the fridge.

NOTE: If you like a stiffer jam, add ½ tablespoon more chia seeds to the strawberry mixture.

MAKES 1 CUP

PREPARATION TIME: 45 minutes

One 10-ounce bag frozen strawberries, thawed

1 tablespoon raw honey

2½ tablespoons chia seeds

1 tablespoon fresh lemon juice or orange blossom water

Coconut, Berry, and Spinach Smoothie

"This has spinach in it?" Pete made my day with his question. Berries, spinach, coconut milk, and egg yolks make a beautiful pink/purple smoothie that's great for those hectic mornings.

SERVES 4

PREPARATION TIME: 5 minutes

1½ cups canned coconut milk

1½ cups frozen blueberries

1½ cups frozen raspberries

1½ cups baby spinach

4 raw egg yolks, from pastured or good-quality organic eggs (see Note)

2 to 3 tablespoons raw honey (I use clover honey) or a few pinches of stevia

Place all ingredients in a blender with 1½ cups cold water and blend until smooth. Adjust the sweetness to taste. Serve.

NOTE: If you're not comfortable consuming raw egg yolks, just omit them.

Fluffy Pancakes

If you want to convince your friends and family that grain-free cooking can be every bit as delicious as cooking with grains, here's your recipe. These pancakes are light and fluffy with a touch of sweetness. Almond flour has a tendency to burn quickly, so it's very important to cook these pancakes over medium-low heat and no higher. Add a bit of whipped cream and a drizzle of maple syrup for the ultimate indulgence on a Saturday morning.

SERVES 6

PREPARATION TIME: 30 minutes
(this is to cook all pancakes)

3 cups almond flour

¼ cup coconut flour

1½ teaspoons unflavored grass-fed gelatin

1 teaspoon baking soda

1½ teaspoons Grain-Free Baking Powder (page 272)

½ teaspoon Celtic sea salt

6 large eggs

1 cup canned coconut milk

2 tablespoons fresh lemon juice

¼ cup coconut or maple sugar

1 tablespoon Pure Vanilla Extract (page 274)

4 tablespoons (½ stick) unsalted butter

1. Whisk the almond flour, coconut flour, gelatin, baking soda, baking powder, and salt in a large mixing bowl. Place the eggs, coconut milk, lemon juice, coconut sugar, and vanilla in a large measuring cup and whisk to combine. Pour the wet ingredients into the dry ingredients and whisk until no lumps remain. Let the batter sit for 5 minutes.

2. Heat a large skillet over medium-low heat for 3 minutes. Add a pat of butter and swirl the pan to coat. Use a ¼-cup scoop to pour the batter into the skillet. Cook until the bottoms of the pancakes are golden brown and the small bubbles that form on top are popping, about 2 minutes. Using a spatula, flip the pancakes and cook the other side until golden brown. Repeat with the remaining butter and batter. Serve.

PALEO/DAIRY-FREE ADAPTATION: Use coconut oil in place of the butter for frying.

NOTE: To change up the flavor of the pancakes, mix in a different extract such as almond or hazelnut. To add nuts or berries, sprinkle them over the batter right after you pour it onto the skillet.

Ham and Egg Cups

This is our new favorite breakfast: baked eggs in a ham cup with leeks and cheese. The ham crisps and creates the perfect shell to hold the runny eggs. If you prefer fully cooked eggs, you can whisk the eggs together before pouring them into the muffin pan. These cups pair well with Berries with Mint (page 45).

SERVES 6
PREPARATION TIME: 25 minutes

Coconut oil for the pan

12 thin slices ham

¼ cup chopped leeks

¼ cup grated Cheddar cheese

12 large eggs

1. Preheat the oven to 375°F and adjust the rack to the middle position. Oil a 12-cup muffin tin.

2. Place a piece of ham in each muffin cup, pushing gently so the ham lines the bottom of the cup. Place 1 teaspoon chopped leeks and 1 teaspoon Cheddar in each cup and crack an egg into each one.

3. Bake for 15 minutes, or until the eggs are set to your liking. Let cool for 3 minutes. Run a large spoon around the edge of each muffin cup and scoop it out of the pan. Serve.

PALEO/DAIRY-FREE ADAPTATION: Omit the cheese.

NOTE: As an alternative, you can use sliced turkey or prosciutto.

Spinach and Sausage Strata

When family and friends come to visit during the holidays, I like to have some make-ahead breakfast dishes ready so I'm not slaving over a hot stove while everyone else relaxes. This strata is a perfect solution. It's all assembled the day before, refrigerated overnight, and then goes straight from the fridge to the oven.

1. Melt the butter in a large sauté pan over medium heat. Swirl to coat the pan. Add the onion and cook until translucent, 5 to 7 minutes. Add the sausage and cook until it's no longer pink, breaking the pork into small pieces with the back of a wooden spoon. Stir in the spinach and cook for 1 or 2 minutes, until hot.

2. In a medium bowl, whisk the milk, eggs, salt, and pepper until combined.

3. Butter an 8 x 8-inch baking dish. Spread half the bread in an even layer over the bottom of the pan. Cover with half the sausage mixture and 1 cup of the cheese. Layer the remaining bread on top and then top with the remaining sausage mixture. Slowly pour the egg mixture over the casserole and sprinkle with the remaining cheese. Cover tightly with plastic wrap and chill the strata overnight in the fridge.

4. Preheat the oven to 325°F and adjust the rack to the middle position. Uncover the strata and bake for 50 to 55 minutes, until the top is golden brown. Let rest for 15 minutes before serving.

PALEO/DAIRY-FREE ADAPTATION: Use 3 tablespoons coconut oil in place of the butter. Use almond milk in place of the whole milk. Omit the cheese.

SERVES 8
PREPARATION TIME: 90 minutes, plus overnight chilling

4 tablespoons (½ stick) unsalted butter, plus more for the baking dish

1 yellow onion, chopped

1 pound pork sausage

5 ounces frozen spinach, thawed and squeezed until almost dry

2 cups milk

8 large eggs

1 teaspoon Celtic sea salt

⅛ teaspoon freshly ground black pepper

1 loaf Grain-Free Bread, cubed (page 266)

2 cups grated Fontina cheese

Egg Scramble with Bacon, Onion, and Swiss Chard

Sometimes eggs can get a little boring, so I like to change them up by adding meats, vegetables, and different cheeses. We had some friends over one weekend, and when their teenage son took a bite of this dish, he said, "Wow. It's like eggs, but better!" That was pretty much the ultimate compliment.

SERVES 6

PREPARATION TIME: 25 minutes

6 bacon slices, chopped

1 large red onion, chopped

4 cups chopped Swiss chard (about ½ bunch)

½ teaspoon Celtic sea salt, plus more to taste

10 large eggs

1 tablespoon heavy cream

1 cup grated Cheddar cheese

1. Cook the bacon in a large skillet over medium heat, stirring frequently, until crispy, about 8 minutes. Using a slotted spoon, transfer the bacon to a plate and set aside. Add the onion, chard, and salt to the skillet and cook, stirring frequently, until the onion is just turning golden brown on the edges, about 10 minutes.

2. Crack the eggs into a large bowl and pour in the cream. Whisk until well combined. Pour the eggs over the onion mixture, add the cooked bacon, and sprinkle with the cheese. Using a spatula, stir the egg mixture until it's scrambled and cooked to your liking. Season to taste with salt. Serve.

PALEO/DAIRY-FREE ADAPTATION: Use canned coconut milk instead of heavy cream. Omit the cheese.

> Even with reasonably priced meat, the cost of feeding a large family can really start to add up. I like to find creative ways to stretch my meats so they go further. We love bacon, but the organic, pastured, uncured kind is pricey. So instead of cooking a few pieces for everyone, I cut the bacon into small pieces, toss it in with a hash or scrambled eggs, and make a package last for four meals instead of one.

Zucchini and Granola Muffins

Zucchini and vanilla-infused granola make for a unique morning combination. I like to freeze these muffins and then reheat them for about 10 minutes at 350°F (no need to thaw). They're a great quick breakfast!

1. Preheat the oven to 375°F and adjust the rack to the middle position. Line a muffin pan with muffin liners.

2. Whisk the eggs, cream, honey, vanilla, and butter in a large mixing bowl. Sift the coconut flour, baking powder, baking soda, and salt into a medium bowl. Stir the zucchini into the flour mixture. Add the wet ingredients to the dry ingredients and whisk until no lumps remain. Fold in the granola.

3. Divide the batter among 18 muffin cups and bake for 18 to 20 minutes, or until lightly browned on top. Store the muffins in an airtight container for up to 3 days.

PALEO/DAIRY-FREE ADAPTATION: Use canned coconut milk in place of the heavy cream. Use 6 tablespoons coconut oil in place of the butter.

NOTE: You can change the flavor of these muffins by using almond extract instead of the vanilla or, for a nut-free variation, omit the granola and use 1 cup frozen blueberries.

MAKES ABOUT 18 MUFFINS

PREPARATION TIME: 30 minutes

6 large eggs

⅓ cups heavy cream

⅓ cup raw honey

1 tablespoon Pure Vanilla Extract (page 274)

8 tablespoons (1 stick) unsalted butter, melted

¾ cup plus 2 tablespoons coconut flour

2 teaspoons Grain-Free Baking Powder (page 272)

1 teaspoon baking soda

½ teaspoon Celtic sea salt

2 cups shredded zucchini

1 cup crumbled Granola (page 227)

Berries with Mint

Any brunch or large breakfast usually includes a bowl of fruit to round out the meal. I like to use fresh berries tossed with mint and lime juice for a change from the usual bananas and oranges. They make for a pretty presentation, too. If you're feeling a bit fancy, you can omit the lime juice and add a splash of orange blossom extract before tossing.

Gently toss the berries, mint, and lime juice in a mixing bowl. Serve.

SERVES 6
PREPARATION TIME: 10 minutes

4 pints mixed berries
¼ cup chopped fresh mint
Juice of 1 lime

Bacon and Cheddar Waffles

These waffles are quite the treat for a morning meal. Salty bits of bacon and creamy Cheddar cheese are enveloped in a crisp waffle. The icing on the cake, so to speak, is the maple syrup. It pulls the entire meal together. We prefer to eat waffles with a bit of butter, so instead of slathering on the butter and then pouring on maple syrup, I pour about ½ cup maple syrup into a small saucepan along with 2 tablespoons butter. I heat the mixture over low heat and stir until combined. Then I have hot buttered maple syrup for pouring. Perfect!

SERVES 4

PREPARATION TIME: 20 minutes

½ cup raw cashews, soaked overnight and drained

1½ cups almond flour

2 tablespoons coconut flour

¾ teaspoon unflavored grass-fed gelatin

½ teaspoon Celtic sea salt

1½ teaspoons baking soda

4 large eggs

4 tablespoons (½ stick) unsalted butter, melted

1 tablespoon raw honey (I use clover)

2 teaspoons apple cider vinegar

6 bacon slices, cooked and crumbled

1 cup shredded Cheddar cheese

Maple syrup for serving

1. Place the cashews and ¼ cup water in the bowl of a food processor. Process until smooth, scraping down the sides a few times to ensure all cashews are pureed. Add the almond flour, coconut flour, gelatin, salt, baking soda, eggs, butter, honey, and cider vinegar and process until smooth.

2. Pour the batter into a large mixing bowl and fold in the bacon and Cheddar. Cook in a waffle maker according to the manufacturer's instructions. Serve with maple syrup.

PALEO/DAIRY-FREE ADAPTATION: Use coconut oil in place of the butter. Omit the cheese.

NOTE: For the classic chicken and waffles, use chicken breasts for the Chicken Nuggets on page 230 and serve on top of these waffles with maple syrup.

Creamed Kale and Eggs

Kale is a great source of fat-soluble vitamins A, C, and K. Fat-soluble vitamins are better utilized by the body when accompanied by fat, so this blend of kale, leeks, butter, and cream is a great way to start your day with the proper fats and nutrients.

SERVES 4
PREPARATION TIME: 25 minutes

4 tablespoons (½ stick) unsalted butter

2 large leeks, trimmed and chopped

1 bunch kale, chopped

½ teaspoon Celtic sea salt

½ cup heavy cream

8 large eggs

Freshly ground black pepper

1. Preheat the oven to 350°F and adjust the rack to the middle position.

2. Melt the butter in a large ovenproof skillet over medium heat and swirl to coat the bottom of the pan. Add the leeks and cook until soft, 3 to 5 minutes. Add the kale and salt and cook for about 5 minutes, stirring occasionally. Stir in the cream and cook for about 1 minute, until hot.

3. Crack the eggs evenly over the kale mixture and place the skillet in the oven. Bake for about 8 minutes, until the whites are cooked but the yolks are still runny. Season with black pepper. Serve immediately.

PALEO/DAIRY-FREE ADAPTATION: Use 2 tablespoons coconut oil in place of the butter. Use canned coconut milk in place of the heavy cream.

Pork Carnitas Breakfast Crepe Tacos

This is a fun breakfast to make when you have some leftover Pork Carnitas (page 176) from the night before. The crepes and dressing can be made a day ahead of time and refrigerated until ready to use. You can substitute shredded cooked chicken or beef for the pork in this recipe to change things up a bit.

1. Puree all the avocado dressing ingredients in a blender. Toss the cabbage, carrots, and cilantro in a bowl.

2. Place a crepe on a plate and top with a spoonful of carnitas and slaw. Drizzle the avocado dressing on top and spritz with lime juice. Repeat with the remaining crepes, slaw, and dressing. Serve immediately.

PALEO/DAIRY-FREE ADAPTATION: Use plain coconut yogurt instead of Greek yogurt.

SERVES 6
PREPARATION TIME: 20 minutes

AVOCADO DRESSING

3 garlic cloves

¼ cup extra-virgin olive oil

1 avocado

2 tablespoons fresh lemon juice

¼ cup Greek yogurt

¾ teaspoon Celtic sea salt

SLAW

2 cups thinly sliced green cabbage

1 cup shredded carrots

¼ cup chopped fresh cilantro

1 recipe Savory Crepes (page 277)

2 cups warmed Pork Carnitas (page 176)

1 lime, cut into wedges

Pumpkin, Currant, and Pecan Breakfast Cookies

Breakfast cookies made with good fats, eggs, nuts, and healthy gelatin are a great, quick way to start the day. I like to make a batch of these on the weekends so we can use them on hurried mornings. They do get a bit soft as the days go by, so if you're in a rush, place them in a 300°F oven for about 8 minutes while you run around and get ready.

MAKES 1 DOZEN 3-INCH COOKIES

PREPARATION TIME: 35 minutes

6 tablespoons unsalted butter, melted

¼ cup raw honey

2 tablespoons pumpkin puree

2 large eggs

1 tablespoon Pure Vanilla Extract (page 274)

2 cups almond flour

2 tablespoons coconut flour

½ teaspoon baking soda

1 teaspoon Celtic sea salt

1 teaspoon ground cinnamon

½ teaspoon unflavored grass-fed gelatin

¼ cup chopped pecans or walnuts

½ cup currants

1. Preheat the oven to 350°F and adjust the rack to the middle position. Line a baking sheet with unbleached parchment paper.

2. In a small bowl, whisk together the butter, honey, pumpkin, eggs, and vanilla. In a large bowl, whisk together the almond flour, coconut flour, baking soda, salt, cinnamon, and gelatin. Add the wet ingredients to the dry ingredients and stir until just combined. Fold in the nuts and currants.

3. Using a 2½-inch cookie scoop, scoop the batter onto the baking sheet to make 12 cookies. Bake for 23 to 25 minutes, or until just golden brown on the edges. Cool on the baking sheet.

PALEO/DAIRY-FREE ADAPTATION: Use 5 tablespoons coconut oil in place of the butter.

Broccoli, Bacon, and Red Onion Frittata

A frittata makes a quick and filling meal any time of day. You can vary the meat and vegetables in this recipe to your taste.

SERVES 6

PREPARATION TIME: 40 minutes

6 bacon slices, cut into small pieces

1 red onion, diced

1 teaspoon Celtic sea salt

2 cups chopped broccoli florets and stems

12 large eggs

2 tablespoons heavy cream

¼ teaspoon freshly ground black pepper

1 cup shredded Havarti or other mild cheese

2 cups arugula (optional)

1. Preheat the oven on the broiler setting and adjust the rack to the middle position.

2. Place the bacon in a large ovenproof skillet and cook over medium heat until crispy, about 5 minutes. Transfer the bacon to a plate, leaving the bacon fat in the skillet. Add the onion to the skillet and season with ½ teaspoon of the salt. Cook for about 20 minutes, until caramelized, stirring occasionally. Add the broccoli and sauté for 2 to 3 minutes, until bright green and still very crunchy. Stir the bacon into the mixture.

3. In a medium bowl, whisk together the eggs, cream, remaining ½ teaspoon salt, and pepper. Pour the eggs over the bacon mixture. Stir the mixture with a spatula, scraping the bottom of the skillet, until large curds form but the eggs are still very wet, about 2 minutes.

4. Sprinkle the eggs with the cheese and place under the broiler until cooked through (the eggs should be firm when you shake the pan) and the cheese is spotty brown, 3 to 4 minutes. Watch carefully so that the cheese doesn't burn. Cut into wedges and top with arugula, if using.

PALEO/DAIRY-FREE ADAPTATION: Use canned coconut milk instead of heavy cream. Omit the cheese.

Coconut Crepes with Whipped Cream and Strawberries

This special-occasion breakfast dish is perfect for birthdays, Mother's Day, or a ladies' brunch. The crepes can be made a couple of days ahead, layered with parchment paper, and stored in an airtight container in the refrigerator. You can change the filling with jams, jellies, yogurt, and different fruits.

1. To make the batter, place the eggs, coconut milk, coconut flour, salt, honey, and melted butter in a blender and blend until smooth. Let the batter sit for 1 hour.

2. Heat a large sauté pan over medium heat until hot, about 2 minutes. Melt 2 teaspoons of the ghee and swirl to coat the pan. Pour ¼ cup of the batter into the pan and swirl to coat. When the bottom of the crepe is golden brown, after just 1 or 2 minutes, flip it using a spatula. Cook until the other side is golden brown. Place the cooked crepe on a baking sheet and repeat with the rest of the batter.

3. To serve, place a cooled crepe on a plate, top with a dollop of whipped cream and a few strawberries, and fold the crepe over.

PALEO/DAIRY-FREE ADAPTATION: Use coconut oil in place of the butter and ghee. Use Whipped Coconut Milk (page 270) in place of the whipped cream.

NOTE: For a savory crepe, omit the honey and add a few tablespoons of chopped herbs to the batter (see page 277). Fill the savory crepe with cheeses, light meats, and a splash of hot sauce.

SERVES 6

PREPARATION TIME: 1½ hours (most of this is chilling time)

CREPE BATTER

6 large eggs

1 cup canned coconut milk

¼ cup coconut flour

½ teaspoon Celtic sea salt

1 tablespoon raw honey

3 tablespoons unsalted butter, melted

CREPES

¼ cup ghee

1 cup heavy cream, whipped

2 cups strawberries, sliced

Cauliflower and Bacon Hash

This is the ultimate replacement for potato hash. The first time I made it my husband was a bit skeptical, but after a few bites he said, "This is amazing!" It pairs well with scrambled or sunny-side-up eggs.

SERVES 4 TO 6

PREPARATION TIME: 15 minutes

6 bacon slices, cut into ¼-inch pieces

1 large yellow onion, chopped

1 recipe "Riced" Cauliflower (page 263)

2 teaspoons Celtic sea salt

Place the bacon in a large skillet over medium heat and fry until golden brown, about 5 minutes. Using a slotted spoon, transfer the bacon to a plate. Add the chopped onion to the bacon fat and sauté until translucent, 4 to 5 minutes. Add the cauliflower and salt. Cook for about 10 minutes, stirring occasionally, until the cauliflower has softened and some pieces are just beginning to turn golden brown on the edges. Stir the bacon into the cauliflower mixture and serve.

Cinnamon Rolls

When I first went grain-free I thought I'd never eat a cinnamon roll again—I actually shed a few tears over the idea. I took my sadness as a challenge and worked for months to create my ideal grain-free cinnamon roll. The result is a soft but sturdy doughy roll swirled with a sugary-cinnamon filling and topped with a white vanilla glaze. The glycemic index for this recipe is a bit on the high side, but for an occasional treat, it hits the spot.

MAKES 8 CINNAMON ROLLS

PREPARATION TIME: 60 minutes

DOUGH

6 tablespoons unsalted butter, melted

2 cups plus 2 tablespoons almond flour

¼ cup tapioca flour

½ cup plus 2 tablespoons arrowroot flour

6 tablespoons coconut flour, plus 1 tablespoon for sprinkling

1¼ teaspoons Grain-Free Baking Powder (page 272)

½ teaspoon baking soda

½ teaspoon Celtic sea salt

2 tablespoons coconut sugar

1 cup canned coconut milk

2 tablespoons fresh lemon juice

SPICE SWIRL

½ cup coconut sugar

1 teaspoon ground cinnamon

¼ teaspoon ground nutmeg

¼ teaspoon Celtic sea salt

2 tablespoons unsalted butter, melted

1. Preheat the oven to 375°F and adjust the rack to the middle position. Using a pastry brush, coat a 9-inch cake pan with 1 tablespoon of the melted butter.

2. To make the spice swirl, in a small bowl, combine the coconut sugar, cinnamon, nutmeg, and salt. Stir in the melted butter until the mixture is damp. Set aside.

3. In a large mixing bowl, whisk together the almond flour, tapioca flour, arrowroot flour, coconut flour, baking powder, baking soda, salt, and coconut sugar. In a measuring glass, whisk together the coconut milk, lemon juice, and 2 tablespoons of the butter. Pour the wet ingredients into the dry ingredients and stir until a rough dough forms. Let the dough sit for 10 minutes.

4. Sprinkle a bit of coconut flour onto a clean work surface. Place the dough on the surface and gently press it into a 12 x 9-inch rectangle. Using a pastry brush, brush the dough with 1 tablespoon of melted butter. Pour the spice swirl mixture over the dough and gently spread it in an even layer. Carefully roll the dough into a 12-inch log (I like to use a bench scaler to lift the dough from the surface). Cut the dough into 8 even pieces. Place the pieces swirl side up in the buttered cake pan and gently press to flatten them to about 1 inch thick. Brush the rolls with the remaining 2 tablespoons of melted butter.

5. Bake for 40 to 45 minutes, or until the rolls are golden brown.

6. To make the icing, in a small saucepan over low heat, combine the coconut butter, honey, vanilla, and ¼ cup plus 2 tablespoons water. Whisk until the icing is a warm, smooth glaze. Drizzle the icing over the rolls. Serve warm.

PALEO/DAIRY-FREE ADAPTATION: Use palm shortening in place of butter.

ICING

½ **cup Coconut Butter (page 273)**

2 tablespoons raw honey

½ **teaspoon Pure Vanilla Extract (page 274)**

Starters

Avocado with Mango-Shrimp Salsa

I love serving this dish during those so-hot-you-can-hardly-breathe days of summer, when there's nothing better than a cool, refreshing mix of seafood, onions, herbs, and fruit, served in a creamy chilled avocado. Add a fresh margarita and you've got the party off to a great start. If you don't want to serve the salsa in an avocado, you can chop up the avocado and toss it in with the salsa. It makes a refreshing side with grilled fish or chicken.

1. Heat the olive oil in a medium sauté pan over medium heat. Swirl the pan to coat. Add the onion and pepper and sauté until soft, about 5 minutes. Add the shrimp and cook until no longer pink, 3 to 4 minutes. Set aside to cool.

2. Toss the mango, cilantro, lime, and jalapeño in a medium bowl. Stir in the cooled shrimp mixture. Scoop a large spoonful of the salsa into each avocado half and serve.

SERVES 8
PREPARATION TIME: 1 hour

1 tablespoon extra-virgin olive oil

½ red onion, finely chopped

1 red, yellow, or orange bell pepper, finely chopped

½ pound raw small or medium shrimp, peeled and deveined

2 mangoes, diced

½ cup chopped fresh cilantro

Juice of 1 lime

1 jalapeño, seeded and chopped

4 avocados, halved and seeded

No-Sugar-Added Margarita

On a hot and humid day down here in the South, nothing is quite as refreshing as a cold margarita. Most margarita recipes contain extra sugars or some sort of mix, but this one is pure and simple. I prefer to use an organic orange liqueur, such as Thatcher's, and a smooth tequila.

SERVES 1

PREPARATION TIME: 5 minutes

Celtic sea salt

Juice of ½ lime

1 ounce good tequila

½ ounce orange liqueur

1. Place two small plates on the counter. Pour a bit of water on one and a ring of salt on the other. Dip the glass into the water and then into the salt.

2. Place 4 large ice cubes in the glass, then pour the lime juice, tequila, and orange liqueur over the ice. Gently stir. Serve.

Seed Crackers

You won't believe how delicious these crackers are! They're salty, crunchy, and nicely flavored with roasted bell pepper. I use them to scoop up all sorts of dips, top them with cheese, or—my kids' favorite—smear a small amount of pastured, organic butter on top.

MAKES 2 LARGE BAKING SHEETS OF CRACKERS
PREPARATION TIME: 10 hours
(almost all of this is dehydrating time)

4 cups sunflower seeds, soaked overnight at room temperature and drained

6 bell peppers, roasted (see below)

1 tablespoon dried Italian seasoning

1 teaspoon Celtic sea salt

6 ounces Pecorino Romano cheese, grated

1. Preheat the oven to 170°F and adjust the rack to the middle position. Line a large baking sheet with unbleached parchment paper.

2. Place the sunflower seeds in the bowl of a food processor and process until finely ground. Add the roasted peppers, Italian seasoning, salt, and cheese. Process until smooth.

3. Using an offset spatula, spread the mixture onto the prepared baking sheet to about ⅛ inch thick. Dehydrate in the oven overnight (7 to 10 hours, depending on how humid your house is) until crisp. Cool to room temperature. Break apart into large crackers and store in an airtight container for up to 2 weeks.

PALEO/DAIRY-FREE ADAPTATION: Omit the cheese.

Roasted Peppers

1. Preheat the broiler with the rack on the highest position. Place the whole peppers on a baking sheet and broil until the skins are just turning black, 2 to 3 minutes. Using a pair of tongs, turn the peppers so the black skin is facing down. Repeat until all sides of the pepper are black.

2. Place the peppers in a deep bowl and cover tightly with plastic wrap. Let the peppers sit for 10 minutes (the steam will loosen the skins). When the peppers are cool enough to handle, peel off the skin and remove the seeds.

Tater Tots

These little bites are pure fun. I like to serve them at kids' parties or when friends come over to watch football. Homemade ranch dressing or ketchup (see pages 256 and 279) is a nice condiment. According to the modern Paleo community, it's okay to eat white potatoes on occasion. They make such a fun treat!

1. Preheat the oven to 375°F and adjust the rack to the middle position.

2. Bake the potatoes uncovered for about 1 hour, or until a knife can be inserted without resistance. Set the potatoes aside to cool.

3. Cut the cooled potatoes into large chunks and press them through a ricer into a large bowl. Discard the skins (or bake them in the oven with a little butter and salt until crispy—a great snack!). Add the arrowroot flour, coconut flour, cheese, salt, and egg to the potatoes and stir until combined. Knead the mixture with your hands until it forms a soft dough. Cover the bowl with a clean towel and let it rest for 15 minutes.

4. Divide the dough into 4 portions and roll each piece into a long rope about 1 inch thick. Cut each rope into 1½-inch-long pieces.

5. Line a baking sheet with paper towels. In a large saucepan, heat 2 inches of tallow or lard to 340°F. Carefully add a third of the tots to the oil and fry, turning the tots as needed, until golden brown on all sides, 3 to 4 minutes. Remove from the oil and place on the prepared baking sheet. Repeat to cook the remaining tots. Sprinkle with salt and serve immediately.

PALEO/DAIRY-FREE ADAPTATION: Omit the cheese.

SERVES 4

PREPARATION TIME: 1 hour 45 minutes (most of this is baking time)

3 large baking potatoes (about 2 pounds), scrubbed

¼ cup plus 2 tablespoons arrowroot flour

2 tablespoons coconut flour

½ cup grated Cheddar cheese

½ teaspoon Celtic sea salt, plus more to taste

1 large egg, beaten

Tallow or lard, for frying

Garlicky Bone Marrow

Buttery, rich, sublime. There really aren't enough words to describe the wonderful flavor of bone marrow. It's my favorite way to start a meal. This recipe comes from my nutritionist and dear friend, Kim. Kim is a simple cook and I love eating at her home. The ingredients are fresh, unadulterated, and nourishing. It's how food should taste.

1. Preheat the oven to 350°F and adjust the rack to the middle position.

2. Place the marrow bones on an oiled cookie sheet or in a baking dish. Sprinkle with the garlic, thyme, and salt. Bake for 15 minutes, or until the marrow in the center is soft. Serve alone or on raw cheese, grain-free bread, or seed crackers.

SERVES 2
PREPARATION TIME: 20 minutes

Ghee or palm shortening for cookie sheet

1 pound marrow bones, preferably grass-fed

1 or 2 garlic cloves, minced

1 teaspoon dried thyme

Coarse Celtic sea salt, to taste

Sausage Cheese Balls

In the South, there was a plate of sausage and cheese balls at every potluck I attended. Remember the ones with sausage and biscuit mix? These little sausage poppers are great for a potluck, game day, or tailgate and are always a hit with the kids.

MAKES 3 DOZEN CHEESE BALLS
PREPARATION TIME: 45 minutes

2½ cups almond flour

1 tablespoon coconut flour

1 teaspoon Celtic sea salt

2 teaspoons Grain-Free Baking Powder (page 272)

½ teaspoon garlic powder

12 ounces Cheddar cheese, shredded

1 pound spicy sausage (pastured and nitrate-free preferred)

1. Preheat the oven to 425°F and adjust the rack to the middle position. Line a baking sheet with unbleached parchment paper.

2. In a large mixing bowl, whisk together the almond flour, coconut flour, salt, baking powder, garlic powder, and cheese. Use your hands to incorporate the sausage into the dry mixture; the mixture will be damp. Roll the mixture into 1½-inch balls and place on the prepared baking sheet. Bake for 25 minutes, until just golden brown. Cool for 5 minutes and serve.

PALEO/DAIRY-FREE ADAPTATION: Omit the cheese. The number of sausage balls will decrease to 18.

Spinach and Roasted Garlic Dip

When football season is in full swing I like to make all sorts of fun foods on game days. Spinach dip, wings, and Zingers (page 81) are my husband's favorites. You can use Seed Crackers (page 68) or an organic potato chip to scoop the dip.

1. Preheat the oven to 350°F and adjust the rack to the middle position.

2. Place a piece of foil on the counter and a piece of unbleached parchment paper on top of the foil. Put the garlic halves on the parchment with the cut cloves facing up, drizzle with olive oil, and fold the parchment and foil around the garlic to make a pouch (keeping the garlic facing up). Bake for 1 hour. When cool enough to handle, squeeze the cloves out of the skins and put them in the bowl of a food processor. Add the remaining dip ingredients and pulse 10 to 15 times, until the mixture is smooth.

3. Pour the mixture into an 8 x 8-inch baking dish and bake for 30 minutes, until bubbly. Serve warm

PALEO/DAIRY-FREE ADAPTATION: Substitute 1½ cups Savory Cashew "Cheese" (page 264) for the cream cheese, sour cream, mayo, and mozzarella. Increase the sea salt to 1 teaspoon and add a few dashes of Tabasco sauce.

SERVES 8

PREPARATION TIME: 2 hours
(most of this is baking time)

1 garlic head, cut in half horizontally

1 tablespoon extra-virgin olive oil

Two 10-ounce packages frozen chopped spinach, thawed

6 ounces cream cheese

¼ cup sour cream

¼ cup mayonnaise

2½ cups grated mozzarella cheese

¼ teaspoon Celtic sea salt

⅛ teaspoon cayenne pepper

Hot Bacon and Mushroom Dip

This recipe comes from my friend Cole Rosenbaum. She has a fabulous catering company, Julia Cole Entertains, in Charlotte, and this is one of her signature dips. It's a smoky, meaty, hearty appetizer that's best served with Seed Crackers (page 68).

SERVES 8 TO 10

PREPARATION TIME: 30 minutes

12 ounces bacon, cut into small pieces

1½ tablespoons extra-virgin olive oil

4 tablespoons (½ stick) unsalted butter or ghee

½ large yellow onion, chopped

1½ teaspoons minced garlic (about 1 clove)

1½ teaspoons Worcestershire sauce

1½ teaspoons fermented tamari sauce

8 ounces white mushrooms, stemmed and chopped

8 ounces cremini mushrooms, stemmed and chopped

½ cup chicken stock

¼ cup white wine (or chicken stock)

1½ teaspoons coconut flour

1 tablespoon Herbamare (see page 14)

1½ teaspoons paprika

2 tablespoons garlic powder

½ teaspoon freshly ground black pepper

4 ounces cream cheese

2 tablespoons sour cream

1. In a large skillet over medium heat, cook the bacon until crispy, 8 to 10 minutes. Using a slotted spoon, transfer the bacon to a small bowl. Pour the bacon fat into a separate bowl and set aside.

2. Heat the olive oil and butter in the same skillet and swirl to coat. Add the onion and garlic and cook for 3 minutes over medium heat, until just beginning to turn translucent. Stir in the Worcestershire sauce and tamari and cook for 1 minute. Stir in the mushrooms, chicken stock, and white wine, bring to a simmer, and cook for 5 minutes, or until the mushrooms are tender. Stir in the coconut flour, Herbamare, paprika, garlic powder, black pepper, cream cheese, sour cream, and crispy bacon and cook, stirring frequently, until all ingredients are incorporated and heated through. Serve the dip hot with crackers.

PALEO/DAIRY-FREE ADAPTATION: Use 3 tablespoons of lard or tallow in place of the butter. Use 1½ teaspoons coconut aminos in place of the tamari and ¾ cup Savory Cashew "Cheese" (page 264) in place of the cream cheese and sour cream. Reduce the Herbamare to 2 teaspoons.

Crispy Sweet Potato Cakes with Cilantro Salsa

These crispy cakes are flat-out fun. Sweet potato "noodle" cakes are fried until crispy and served with a vibrant cilantro and lime salsa. They can be made one hour before serving and kept warm in a 200°F oven.

1. To make the cilantro salsa, combine the garlic and lime juice in a medium bowl. Let the mixture sit for 20 minutes (this will mellow the spiciness of the raw garlic). Stir in the cilantro and salt.

2. Place the potatoes, scallions, eggs, tapioca flour, coconut flour, salt, and 1 cup of the cilantro salsa in a large bowl. Toss well to combine.

3. Preheat the oven to 200°F and set a cooling rack on top of a baking sheet.

4. Heat the tallow in a large skillet over medium-high heat. Swirl the pan to coat. Drop ¼ cup mounds of the sweet potato mixture into the hot tallow, gently pressing with a spatula to flatten to a disk. Fry until the bottom is golden brown, about 2 minutes. Using a spatula, turn the sweet potato cakes and cook the other side until golden brown. Place the cakes on the prepared cooling rack and put the baking sheet in the oven to keep warm. Repeat to make the rest of the sweet potato cakes. Serve warm with the remaining cilantro salsa.

SERVES 6
PREPARATION TIME: 1 hour

CILANTRO SALSA

4 garlic cloves, minced

¼ cup fresh lime juice

2 large bunches of cilantro, chopped

½ teaspoon Celtic sea salt

SWEET POTATO CAKES

3 large sweet potatoes, sliced with a vegetable "spiralizer" (see page 22) or julienne peeler

4 scallions, chopped

2 large eggs, beaten

2 teaspoons tapioca flour

1 teaspoon coconut flour

1 teaspoon Celtic sea salt

1 cup tallow or lard

"Cheesy" Kale Chips

I have yet to find someone who doesn't like a kale chip. And now, layered in creamy cashew "cheese," these kale chips go to a whole new level. A British friend, who was new to the United States, stopped by when I was making these one day and I served her a sample. She said they were delicious and asked, "What cheese are you using in this recipe? It's the best cheese I've had since I've been in America." Needless to say she was shocked when I told her the "cheese" was made from cashews. So I think it's safe to say your guests will probably be fooled, too.

SERVES 6

PREPARATION TIME: 3 hours
(almost all of this is dehydrating time)

1 bunch of kale, torn into large pieces

1 recipe Savory Cashew "Cheese"
(page 264)

1. Preheat the oven to 170°F or as low as your oven will go. Line a baking sheet with unbleached parchment paper.

2. Place the kale in a large mixing bowl and spoon the cashew cheese over the kale. Using your hands, toss the kale until all pieces are coated with cashew mixture. Spread the kale pieces on the prepared baking sheet. Place the kale in the oven and dehydrate for 2½ to 3 hours, or until dry. Cool to room temperature and serve. Store in an airtight container at room temperature for up to 10 days.

Zingers

If you're going to make anything in this book, make this recipe. My mom, owner of The Festive Kitchen, in Dallas, Texas, is the creator of these little bites and sells thirty thousand pounds of them each holiday season. The apricot has a melty-sweet quality, there's a small bite from the jalapeño, and it's all wrapped in salty bacon. It's truly the ultimate appetizer.

1. Preheat the oven to 400°F and adjust the rack to the middle position. Line a baking sheet with unbleached parchment paper.

2. Using a paring knife, cut a slice horizontally down an apricot. Cut almost but not all the way through, so that it will open like a book. Place a jalapeño slice inside the apricot, wrap the apricot in a piece of the cut bacon, secure it with a toothpick, and place it on the prepared baking sheet. Repeat with remaining ingredients.

3. Bake for 10 minutes. Using a pair of tongs, flip the zingers and bake for 10 minutes more, or until the bacon is golden brown. Serve immediately.

NOTE: You can make these ahead of time and freeze them, unbaked, in an airtight container. No need to thaw them—you can bake them straight from the freezer. Just increase the baking time to 25 to 30 minutes.

MAKES 20 APPETIZERS
PREPARATION TIME: 30 minutes

20 dried apricots
20 jarred jalapeño slices
7 bacon slices, cut into thirds
20 strong toothpicks

Fighter Pilot Loaded Fries

My husband is a fighter pilot for the U.S. Air Force, and every fighter pilot squadron has a bar for sharing good times and drinks after a long day. It's a place where families gather on Fridays to hang out, get to know one another, and build camaraderie. Fighter pilots also have a traditional food: jalapeño popcorn. They fry jalapeños with the popcorn so the snack is spicy, and the little bits of salty-crunchy jalapeños are coveted. So, since popcorn is a grain, at our house we like to fry up russet potatoes with jalapeños and top them off with cheese, bacon, and all the fixin's. It's one of my husband's football-watching favorites.

SERVES 6

PREPARATION TIME: 4 hours
(most of this is chilling time)

**4 baking potatoes,
cut into small wedges**

4 cups tallow or lard

1 cup pickled jalapeños

4 cups Cheddar cheese

**6 ounces bacon, cooked
and crumbled**

4 scallions, chopped

1. Place the potatoes in a large bowl and cover with cold water. Refrigerate for at least 3 hours and no longer than 5. Drain and pat dry with a clean dish towel.

2. Preheat the oven to 350°F and adjust the rack to the middle position. Set a cooling rack over a baking sheet.

3. In a large pot or Dutch oven, heat the tallow or lard over medium-high heat until it reaches 340°F. Working in batches, fry the potatoes for 3 minutes (they won't be fully cooked at this point). Place the fried potatoes on the cooling rack. Repeat the process for a second round of frying, this time frying the potatoes for 3 to 4 minutes, until golden brown and crispy.

4. Fry the jalapeños for 2 to 3 minutes, until golden brown.

5. Spread the potatoes in an even layer on a baking sheet. Top with the cheese, bacon, scallions, and jalapeños and bake for 10 to 12 minutes, or until the cheese is melted and bubbly. Serve.

PALEO/DAIRY-FREE ADAPTATION: Omit the cheese.

Egg Salad in Bacon Cups

Strips of bacon baked in muffin cups are a nice grain-free vessel for a small portion of dip or salad to be served as an appetizer. These little cups also make a nice afternoon snack or addition to brunch.

1. Preheat the oven to 350°F and adjust the rack to the middle position.

2. Turn a mini muffin pan upside down and place 3 pieces of bacon on each muffin cup, in a criss-cross pattern. Place another inverted mini muffin pan on top and press firmly. Place both muffin pans on a large baking sheet (if it doesn't fit flat, it's okay). Bake for 35 minutes and set aside to cool completely. Remove the top muffin pan and gently remove the bacon cups.

3. Chop the eggs and place them in a medium bowl. Add the lemon juice, Dijon, mayonnaise, celery, and salt and mix until blended. Spoon the egg salad into the bacon cups, garnish with chives if desired, and serve.

MAKES 16 APPETIZERS
PREPARATION TIME: 1 hour 20 minutes
(most of this is baking or cooling time)

1 pound bacon, each strip cut into thirds

6 large eggs, hard-boiled and chilled (see sidebar)

Juice of ½ lemon

2 teaspoons Dijon mustard

2 tablespoons mayonnaise

¼ cup chopped celery

½ teaspoon Celtic sea salt

2 tablespoons minced fresh chives (optional)

HARD-BOILED EGGS

Place 6 eggs in a medium saucepan and cover with water by 1 inch. Bring the water to a boil over high heat and continue to boil for 1 minute. Remove the pot from the heat, cover with a lid, and let the eggs sit in the hot water for 15 minutes. Transfer the eggs to a bowl of ice water to cool, then drain and refrigerate until ready to use.

Thyme and Cheddar Crackers

A glass of good organic wine and a few crackers is always a nice way to begin a dinner party. These also make a great snack or addition to brunch.

MAKES ABOUT 3 DOZEN CRACKERS

PREPARATION TIME: 1 hour
(most of this is chilling time)

2 cups almond flour

¼ cup coconut flour

½ teaspoon unflavored grass-fed gelatin

1 teaspoon Celtic sea salt

2 tablespoons fresh thyme leaves

½ cup grated Cheddar cheese

6 tablespoons cold unsalted butter, cut into tablespoons

Herbamare (see page 14) for sprinkling (or your favorite organic all-purpose seasoning mix)

1. Place the almond flour, coconut flour, gelatin, salt, thyme, and cheese in the bowl of a food processor and pulse 2 or 3 times to combine. Add the butter and pulse for eight 1-second pulses, then leave the processor on until the dough forms a ball. Transfer the dough onto a large piece of plastic wrap and shape it into a 1½-inch log. Wrap tightly and chill in the refrigerator for at least 30 minutes and up to 2 weeks.

2. Preheat the oven to 350°F and adjust the rack to the middle position. Line a baking sheet with unbleached parchment paper.

3. Remove the dough from the wrap and cut into ¼-inch-thick slices. Lay the slices on the lined baking sheet and bake for 11 minutes, or until just golden brown on the edges. Spinkle with Herbamare right when they come out of the oven. Cool completely. Serve.

PALEO/DAIRY-FREE ADAPTATION: Use 1 teaspoon nutritional yeast in place of the cheese. Use ¼ cup coconut oil in place of the butter.

Antipasti Bites

Little cups of baked salami or pepperoni make a cute vessel for olives, vegetables, herbs, and cheese. The recipe can be made a day ahead of time, but wait to put the chopped vegetable mixture into the baked salami or pepperoni until ready to serve.

1. Preheat the oven to 350°F and adjust the rack to the middle position.

2. Carefully press each salami or pepperoni slice into a mini muffin cup (the sides will crumple up a bit). Bake for 15 minutes. Cool completely.

3. Meanwhile, in a small bowl, toss the roasted pepper, mozzarella, olives, parsley, and olive oil. Season with salt and pepper.

4. Spoon a small portion of the bell pepper mixture into each salami cup. Serve.

PALEO/DAIRY-FREE ADAPTATION: Omit the mozzarella.

SERVES 6 TO 8
PREPARATION TIME: 25 minutes

24 pepperoni or salami slices

1 roasted bell pepper, skinned, seeded, and chopped (see page 68)

¼ cup diced fresh mozzarella

¼ cup chopped black olives

2 tablespoons chopped fresh parsley

1 teaspoon extra-virgin olive oil

Celtic sea salt and freshly ground black pepper

Salads

Eating organic produce is beneficial for your health. While many scientists argue that conventional produce isn't harmful, Dr. Mark Donohoe, a general physician from Sydney, Australia, with a special interest in environmental science, claims they are overlooking other important differences. "Scientists have always said eating organic food is senseless and makes no difference as pesticides don't harm humans; however, the pesticides kill certain species of gut bacteria, not us," Dr. Donohoe told *The Australian.* The immune system is centered in the gut, so it's important to eat foods that promote the health of gut flora instead of destroying it.

A decade ago I was struggling with chronic migraines. I spent more than a year fighting them with several different medications daily and I was beginning to feel helpless. But I discovered the migraines were from the pesticides and herbicides in the foods I was eating.

As soon as I switched to organic, my migraines disappeared and I was able to get off all my daily medications. So as you see, organic foods can play a huge role in your health.

If you're just beginning, make shopping for clean produce easier by memorizing or writing out the Dirty Dozen and Clean Fifteen list, published by the Environmental Working Group (see below). And remember, take it slow and make one change a week, starting with the Dirty Dozen Plus (the list now has fourteen items). If you eat lots of apples, for example, switch to organic apples this week. And next week, maybe start buying organic potatoes. After several months of this approach, most of the produce you purchase will be organic.

DIRTY DOZEN PLUS

Apples	Peaches
Celery	Potatoes
Cherry tomatoes	Spinach
Cucumbers	Strawberries
Grapes	Bell peppers
Hot peppers	Kale and collard greens
Nectarines	Summer squash

CLEAN 15

Asparagus	Mangoes
Avocados	Mushrooms
Cabbage	Onions
Cantaloupe	Papayas
Sweet corn	Pineapples
Eggplant	Sweet peas
Grapefruit	Sweet potatoes
Kiwi	

Salmon, Avocado, and Chickpea Salad, 93

Steak and Romaine Salad with Red Pepper Dressing, 94

Baby Greens, Avocado, Red Onion, and Strawberry Salad, 97

Bacon, Lettuce, and Tomato Salad with a Fried Egg, 98

Arugula Salad, 101

Shrimp Salad with Cilantro-Lime Dressing, 102

Mixed Greens Salad with Chicken, Peaches, and Stilton, 104

Blueberry and Fennel Salad, 107

Cauliflower "Rice" Salad with Herbs and Dried Fruit, 108

Pecan Chicken Salad with Squash, Pears, and Goat Cheese, 110

Citrus Salad with Shallots and Pistachios, 111

Salmon, Avocado, and Chickpea Salad

When you want to eat a light meal, but also get some healthy fats in the mix, this salad is a great choice. The wild salmon contains healthy omega-3 fatty acids and the olive oil and avocado give you a modest dose of unsaturated fats. You can switch out the chickpeas for white navy or cannellini beans or even toss in some arugula for a nice peppery bite.

1. Preheat the oven to 400°F and adjust the rack to the middle position. Line a baking sheet with unbleached parchment paper.

2. Place the salmon on the lined baking sheet. Pat dry with a paper towel and season with salt and pepper. Roast for 8 to 10 minutes, or until cooked through. Set aside to cool.

3. Whisk the olive oil, lemon juice, and Dijon in a small bowl. Combine the greens, chickpeas, avocado, cilantro, and scallions in a large salad bowl. Pour the dressing on top and toss well but gently. Season to taste with salt and pepper. Divide the salad among 4 plates and top each salad with a piece of fish. Serve

PALEO/DAIRY-FREE ADAPTATION: Omit the chickpeas.

SERVES 4

PREPARATION TIME: 30 minutes

1 pound wild salmon fillet, cut into 4 pieces

Celtic sea salt and freshly ground black pepper

3 tablespoons extra-virgin olive oil

Juice of 1 lemon

1 teaspoon Dijon mustard

5 ounces mixed baby greens

1 cup cooked (soaked overnight at room temperature, drained, and simmered until soft) or drained canned chickpeas

2 avocados, sliced

¼ cup chopped fresh cilantro

3 scallions, white and green parts, chopped

Steak and Romaine Salad with Red Pepper Dressing

A creamy dressing of homemade mayonnaise and red bell pepper is the shining star in this salad. Raw garlic can be very spicy in a dressing, but soaking the garlic in lemon juice tames the sharpness. It's a great trick to use when making other raw salad dressings.

SERVES 4

PREPARATION TIME: 35 minutes

STEAK

1 tablespoon ghee

1 pound sirloin (you can also use rib eye or tenderloin)

Celtic sea salt

RED PEPPER DRESSING

2 garlic cloves, minced

Juice of 1 lemon

2 large egg yolks

½ teaspoon Dijon mustard

¼ teaspoon Celtic sea salt, plus more to taste

1 roasted red bell pepper, skinned and seeded (see page 68)

1 cup extra-virgin olive oil

SALAD

1 large head of romaine lettuce, torn into bite-size pieces

2 cups arugula leaves

1 cucumber, chopped

1 cup small cubes of Fontina cheese

½ cup sunflower seed kernels, toasted (see Note)

1. Heat a large skillet over medium-high heat for 1 minute. Add the ghee and swirl to coat. Season both sides of the sirloin with salt and place the steak in the pan. Cook for about 3 minutes, or until the bottom is brown on the edges. Using a pair of tongs, flip the steak and continue to cook until the second side is golden brown or to the desired doneness. Remove and set aside.

2. To make the dressing, combine the garlic and lemon juice in a small bowl and let sit for 10 minutes. Place the egg yolks, Dijon, salt, bell pepper, and lemon-garlic mixture in a food processor or blender and blend for 30 seconds. With the processor running, very slowly add the olive oil (it should take about 1 minute to add all the oil). Pour the dressing into a bowl and season to taste with salt.

3. Thinly slice the steak against the grain. Place the romaine, arugula, cucumber, Fontina, and sunflower seeds in a large salad bowl. Drizzle ½ cup of the dressing over the salad and toss well. Add more dressing if desired. Store leftover dressing in the refrigerator for up to 5 days. Adjust the seasonings to taste and serve.

PALEO/DAIRY-FREE ADAPTATION: Use coconut oil instead of ghee. Omit the cheese.

NOTE: Toast the sunflower seeds over medium heat until just turning golden.

Baby Greens, Avocado, Red Onion, and Strawberry Salad

Red onion can have quite a bite to it, but that sharpness is tempered if you soak the onion in cold water first. I prepare onions this way and my kids will eat them in just about any dish I prepare.

1. Place the onion in a small bowl, cover with cold water, and let rest for about 10 minutes.

2. Meanwhile, in another small bowl, whisk the orange juice, lime juice, honey, Dijon, and salt. Whisk in the olive oil. Adjust the seasonings as desired.

3. Drain the onion and put it in a large salad bowl with the baby greens, avocado, strawberries and orange segments. Pour the dressing on top and toss to coat the leaves. Sprinkle with walnuts, if using.

NOTE: To add some variety to this salad you can toss in some cold, steamed shrimp, use blackberries in place of the strawberries, or use pecans in place of the walnuts.

SERVES 4
PREPARATION TIME: 20 minutes

SALAD

1 small red onion, sliced thin

5 ounces baby greens

2 avocados, sliced thin

1 cup sliced strawberries

2 navel oranges, segmented

¼ cup chopped walnuts (optional)

DRESSING

¼ cup freshly squeezed orange juice

Juice of 1 lime

1½ tablespoons raw honey
(I use clover)

½ teaspoon Dijon mustard

¼ teaspoon Celtic sea salt

3 tablespoons extra-virgin olive oil

Bacon, Lettuce, and Tomato Salad with a Fried Egg

I think almost any dish tastes better when you put an egg on top, especially salad. While many people are afraid of egg yolks, they're actually the most nutritious part of the egg and shouldn't be tossed away. Pastured egg yolks contain high amounts of choline, healthy cholesterol, vitamin A, and other minerals. Go ahead, they're good for you!

SERVES 4

PREPARATION TIME: 20 minutes

8 ounces mixed baby greens

1 cup cherry tomatoes, halved

4 bacon slices, cut into small pieces

1 shallot, minced

1 teaspoon smooth Dijon mustard

1 tablespoon raw apple cider vinegar

1 to 2 tablespoons extra-virgin olive oil, to taste

Celtic sea salt and freshly ground black pepper

1 tablespoon unsalted butter or coconut oil

4 large eggs

1. Place the greens and tomatoes in a large salad bowl. Cook the bacon in a large skillet over medium heat until crispy, about 5 minutes. Using a slotted spoon, transfer the bacon to a small plate. Add the shallot to the skillet and sauté for about 3 minutes, until it just begins to turn golden brown. Stir in the Dijon, vinegar, and olive oil. Stir in the bacon and season with salt and pepper. Pour this dressing into a heat-proof bowl or pitcher.

2. Melt the butter in the now-empty skillet and swirl to coat. Crack in the eggs and fry until the whites are cooked, 1 or 2 minutes.

3. Pour the dressing over the salad and toss. Divide among 4 plates and place a fried egg on top of each salad. Serve.

Arugula Salad

Arugula makes for an easy, last-minute kind of salad. Toss everything together and you're done! You can add shredded carrots or onions to vary the salad a bit. Pine nuts would also be a nice addition.

Place the arugula in a large bowl. Dress with the lemon juice and olive oil and season with salt and pepper. Toss well. Add more salt and pepper to taste.

NOTE: Arugula also does well with creamy dressings such as ranch, Caesar, or blue cheese. I encourage you to start using it in place of your "normal" lettuce to increase the nutritional value of your salad.

SERVES 4

PREPARATION TIME: 10 minutes

1 large bunch (4 ounces) of arugula

Juice of ½ lemon

2 tablespoons extra-virgin olive oil

Celtic sea salt and freshly ground black pepper

Shrimp Salad with Cilantro-Lime Dressing

Wild shrimp are a great source of iodine as well as selenium and calcium. When I was healing from thyroid disease my nutritionist suggested I eat at least two servings of wild seafood every week to help support the thyroid. When shopping for shrimp, make sure to look for wild-caught, since the farmed variety can be raised using chemicals and antibiotics.

There will be some dressing left over. It makes a great dip for vegetables or a sauce to spoon over grilled meat. If you don't have pumpkin seeds on hand you can substitute walnuts or pine nuts.

SERVES 4

PREPARATION TIME: 20 minutes

SALAD

1 tablespoon ghee, lard, or tallow

1 pound shrimp, deveined

Celtic sea salt

1 large head of romaine lettuce, torn into bite-size pieces

2 carrots, shredded

1 bell pepper, cut into bite-size pieces

DRESSING

2 cups firmly packed fresh cilantro leaves

2 garlic cloves

1 cup pumpkin seeds

2 tablespoons fresh lime juice

2 teaspoons Celtic sea salt

1 cup plus 1 to 2 tablespoons extra-virgin olive oil

1. Heat the ghee in a large skillet over medium heat. Add the shrimp, season with salt, and cook for 5 minutes, stirring often, until the shrimp are pink and cooked through. Using a slotted spoon, transfer the shrimp to a bowl.

2. Process all the dressing ingredients in a food processor or blender. If the dressing is too thick, add a bit more oil to thin it to the desired consistency.

3. Place the shrimp, romaine, carrots, and bell pepper in a large salad bowl. Pour ½ cup dressing over the salad and toss well. Store any leftover dressing in an airtight container in the refrigerator for up to 1 week.

Mixed Greens Salad with Chicken, Peaches, and Stilton

Every summer I wait for that moment. The moment when you find the perfectly ripe, sweet peach and as you eat it the juices run down your chin, but you don't care because the fruit is so ripe and so perfect. It's my favorite food moment of the summer. After I find that perfect peach, I find ways to incorporate peaches into my meals. Blue cheese, pecans, and peaches covered in a citrus vinaigrette is the epitome of summer.

SERVES 4

PREPARATION TIME: 50 minutes
(most of this is roasting time)

SALAD

3 bone-in, skin-on chicken breasts

Celtic sea salt and freshly ground black pepper

8 ounces mixed baby greens

2 peaches, pitted and cut into wedges

½ cup pecans

¼ cup crumbled Stilton cheese

DRESSING

3 tablespoons fresh lime juice

5 tablespoons fresh orange juice

1 teaspoon Dijon mustard

1 teaspoon plain Greek yogurt

1 teaspoon raw honey

⅓ cup extra-virgin olive oil

1½ teaspoons poppy seeds

1. Preheat the oven to 400°F and adjust the rack to the middle position.

2. Place the chicken breasts skin side up on a baking sheet and season with salt and pepper. Roast for 35 minutes, until golden brown and cooked through. When cool enough to handle, remove the skin and shred the chicken or cut it into bite-size pieces.

3. Place the baby greens, peaches, pecans, Stilton, and chicken in a large salad bowl.

4. Whisk the lime juice, orange juice, mustard, yogurt, honey, olive oil, and poppy seeds together and pour over the salad. Toss. Serve immediately.

PALEO/DAIRY-FREE ADAPTATION: Omit the Stilton. Use the thick coconut cream that rises to the top of a can of coconut milk in place of the Greek yogurt.

Blueberry and Fennel Salad

This recipe was inspired by a cooking class I took with Chef Andrew Cooper at the Four Seasons Santa Fe. Chef Andrew advocates using the whole plant or animal—root to leaves, nose to tail. He talked about using the leaves and stalks from the vegetables in our refrigerator that we usually throw away. This salad utilizes the fennel fronds and bright green celery leaves (found on the inside of a stalk of celery) to make a vibrant summer salad.

Toss all the ingredients in a salad bowl. Serve cold.

SERVES 6
PREPARATION TIME: 20 minutes

NOTE: If you like things on the sweeter side, you can drizzle a bit of honey over the salad and toss.

3 ounces pancetta, cooked and crumbled

1 fennel bulb, sliced thin

¼ cup chopped fennel fronds (the little leaves on the end of the fennel stalk)

¼ cup celery leaves

12 ounces blueberries

1 tablespoon extra-virgin olive oil

Grated zest and juice of 1 lemon

Grated zest and juice of 1 orange

Dash of chili flakes

⅛ teaspoon Celtic sea salt

Cauliflower "Rice" Salad with Herbs and Dried Fruit

While experimenting with cauliflower, I discovered that you can use it as a pasta or wild rice substitute in just about any dish. It's crunchy and has a mild enough flavor that most people who taste it actually think it's rice. This is an easy, laid-back side dish that pairs nicely with poultry and beef but also works well as a light lunch. You can change the fruit (I particularly like dried cranberries or dried blueberries) and add some seeds or maybe even a bit of goat cheese to suit your taste. It's best served at room temperature.

SERVES 6

PREPARATION TIME: 20 minutes

1 tablespoon unsalted butter or coconut oil

1 onion, chopped

1 recipe "Riced" Cauliflower (page 263)

1 cup chopped fresh parsley leaves

½ cup chopped fresh mint leaves

1 cup chopped fresh cilantro leaves

3 tablespoons fresh lemon juice

¼ cup extra-virgin olive oil

½ teaspoon Celtic sea salt, plus more to taste

1 cup chopped dried apricots

1 cup chopped walnuts

1. Melt the butter in a medium sauté pan over medium heat. Swirl to coat. Add the onion and cook until soft, about 5 minutes. Add the "riced" cauliflower to the onion and cook, stirring frequently, until warm but still crunchy, about 2 minutes.

2. Transfer the onion and cauliflower mixture to a large salad bowl. Add the parsley, mint, cilantro, lemon juice, olive oil, salt, apricots, and walnuts. Toss 10 to 15 times to mix well. Adjust the salt to taste. Serve at room temperature.

NOTE: At the holidays you can substitute cranberries for the apricots and pistachios for the walnuts for a festive red and green look.

Pecan Chicken Salad with Squash, Pears, and Goat Cheese

When fall comes, I enjoy using a variety of squash, nuts, and cheeses in our salads. The butternut squash cubes turn into sweet little gems when caramelized in ghee. You can substitute apples or ripe figs for the pears.

SERVES 4

PREPARATION TIME: 30 minutes

4 boneless, skinless chicken breasts, pounded thin

Celtic sea salt and freshly ground black pepper

1 cup pecans, pulsed in a food processor until finely ground

2 large eggs

¼ cup ghee, lard, or tallow

2 cups ¼-inch dice butternut squash

5 ounces mixed greens

2 pears, cut into bite-size pieces

¼ cup crumbled goat cheese

¼ cup extra-virgin olive oil

2 tablespoons balsamic vinegar

1. Season the chicken breasts with salt and pepper. Place the ground pecans in a shallow dish. Crack the eggs in a pie plate and beat with 1 tablespoon water. Heat 2 tablespoons of the ghee in a large skillet over medium-high heat. Dredge each piece of chicken in the egg and then in the pecans, then immediately place the chicken in the pan. Cook for 3 to 4 minutes, until the bottom is golden brown. Using tongs, carefully flip the chicken and cook until the other side is golden brown and the chicken is cooked through, about 4 minutes. Let the chicken cool while you make the rest of the salad.

2. Put the remaining 2 tablespoons ghee and the squash in the pan. Cook over medium heat for 10 minutes, stirring every 3 minutes or so, until the squash is soft and just turning golden brown on the edges. Place the squash in a large salad bowl and cool for 10 minutes.

3. Add the greens, pears, and goat cheese to the salad bowl. Drizzle the olive oil and balsamic vinegar on top, season with a bit of salt, and toss. Serve with the chicken.

Citrus Salad with Shallots and Pistachios

A plate of bright citrus fruits adds some welcome color and a burst of fresh flavors during the cold days of winter. You can use any combination of citrus you like in this salad, including clementines, Mineola oranges, and tangelos.

Arrange the grapefruit and orange slices on a round platter. Combine the shallot and lemon juice in a small bowl and let sit for 10 minutes. Whisk in the honey and olive oil. Drizzle the dressing over the citrus fruits and sprinkle with the pistachios and salt.

SERVES 6

PREPARATION TIME: 15 minutes

2 grapefruit, cut into ¼-inch slices

3 oranges, cut into ¼-inch slices

3 blood oranges, cut into ¼-inch slices

1 shallot, minced (about ¼ cup)

1 tablespoon fresh lemon juice

1 teaspoon raw honey

3 tablespoons extra-virgin olive oil

½ cup chopped pistachios

⅛ teaspoon coarse Celtic sea salt

Sides

I love to entertain, but it can be stressful. I used to toil in the kitchen all day before the guests came, only to want to crawl into bed by the time they arrived. This all changed when our family began eating grain free. All of a sudden I found cooking to be simple and much less time consuming. Cooking large dinners for friends and family wasn't so difficult anymore. When you remove the breads and pastas, the door opens to flavorful roasted meats and vegetables, hearty salads, fruits, fresh cheeses, and puddings. These foods are easy to prepare with few ingredients, which means easy, low-stress entertaining.

I try to keep the menu simple. For example, I'll make a roasted chicken with roasted vegetables and a hearty salad. Anything roasted is perfect for entertaining because you put it in the oven and let the heat do its magic. Salads are easy to prepare and can be changed with the seasons. I usually make a dessert that can be prepared the day before, such as a pudding or ice cream.

In the winter I like to pair a roast with root vegetables and baked pears. In the spring it's a roasted chicken with a light and colorful salad and a coconut cake with buttercream frosting. In the summer, I pick up whatever fish looks best at the market and let my husband, Pete, grill outside. I pair that with fresh tomatoes, blanched green beans, and ice cream for dessert. In the fall I pull out the slow cooker for pork carnitas, pair it with squash and greens, then finish the meal with a pie or crisp.

I think the best idea is to choose a few things to serve, but make those foods right. Use the best cut of meats you can afford and the freshest seasonings you can find. Shop at your local farmer's market for ripe produce, or grow some of your own vegetables in your backyard. Good salt, freshly cracked pepper, a good olive oil, fresh cream—these ingredients are the details that make a huge difference.

Sautéed Bell Peppers with Chimichurri Sauce

Chimichurri makes a nice complement to sautéed or grilled vegetables, meats, or even scrambled eggs. It's a recipe you can easily adapt to your taste. If you like a bit more spice, add some serrano peppers or other chiles. If you have extra herbs in the garden add them—a bit of cilantro or basil would work nicely.

Heat the 1 tablespoon oil in a large skillet over medium heat. Add the bell peppers and sauté for 5 to 7 minutes, until they are soft and some of the edges just begin to brown. Place the parsley, garlic, jalapeño, and oregano in a medium bowl and stir in the vinegar, salt, and ½ cup olive oil. Pour the sauce over the peppers and serve.

SERVES 4

PREPARATION TIME: 10 minutes

½ cup plus 1 tablespoon extra-virgin olive oil

4 large red, yellow, or orange bell peppers, cut into ½-inch slices

1 cup fresh flat-leaf parsley leaves, finely chopped

3 garlic cloves, finely chopped

½ jalapeño, seeded and finely chopped (optional)

2 fresh oregano sprigs, leaves finely chopped

¼ cup sherry vinegar

¼ teaspoon Celtic sea salt

Butternut Squash, Zucchini, and Tomato Gratin

I love the presentation of this gratin—small vegetable slices lined up to create a dish that's as colorful as it is delicious. You can swap the vegetables in this dish for potatoes or other types of squash, or use shallots instead of onions for a more delicate flavor. The dish can be composed a day ahead, covered, and stored in the refrigerator until ready to bake.

SERVES 4

PREPARATION TIME: 1 hour

2 tablespoons unsalted butter

2 large yellow onions, thinly sliced

½ teaspoon dried thyme

1 medium butternut squash, quartered lengthwise, peeled, and cut into ¼-inch-thick slices

3 zucchini, cut into ¼-inch-thick slices

3 tomatoes, cut into ¼-inch-thick slices

½ teaspoon Celtic sea salt

½ cup grated Pecorino Romano cheese

1. Preheat the oven to 350°F and adjust the rack to the middle position.

2. Heat the butter in a large skillet over medium heat. Add the onions and cook, stirring occasionally, until caramelized, about 12 minutes. Stir in the thyme and cook until fragrant, about 45 seconds. Spread the onions evenly in a 10-inch round baking dish.

3. Layer the vegetables over the onions, alternating the squash, zucchini, and tomatoes until you've used them all. Cover the dish with unbleached parchment paper and then a piece of foil (this keeps the foil from touching the food while it bakes). Bake for 15 minutes. Remove the parchment and foil. Sprinkle with the salt and cheese. Bake for 15 to 20 minutes, until bubbling.

PALEO/DAIRY-FREE ADAPTATION: Use coconut oil in place of the butter. Use 2 tablespoons nutritional yeast in place of the cheese.

Green Beans with Onion and Ham

There's nothing fancy about this dish. It's perfect on a lazy weekend served alongside roasted meat and maybe a baked potato.

Melt the butter in a medium saucepan over medium heat and swirl to coat. Add the onion and cook, stirring occasionally, until soft, about 5 minutes. Add the green beans, ham hock, stock, salt, and granulated garlic. Reduce the heat to a simmer and cook for 20 minutes, until the beans are soft and have taken on the ham and garlic flavor. Season with salt to taste. Serve.

PALEO/DAIRY-FREE ADAPTATION: Use coconut oil in place of the butter.

SERVES 4

PREPARATION TIME: 30 minutes

2 tablespoons unsalted butter

1 onion, chopped

One 16-ounce bag frozen green beans (or 1 pound fresh beans)

2 ounces ham hock or seasoned pork

1 cup Chicken Stock (page 252)

1 teaspoon Celtic sea salt, plus more to taste

1½ teaspoons granulated garlic

Sweet Buttered Peas
with Orange and Mint Gremolata

A side dish doesn't need to be complicated. Sweet peas, chicken stock, butter, and mint make for an easy and casual accompaniment for any night of the week.

Place the peas and stock in a medium saucepan. Bring to a simmer over medium heat and cook until the peas are tender, about 8 minutes. Add the butter and stir until melted. Stir the zest, mint, and garlic into the peas. Season to taste with salt and pepper.

PALEO/DAIRY-FREE ADAPTATION: Use 1 tablespoon palm shortening in place of the butter.

SERVES 4
PREPARATION TIME: 10 minutes

One 10-ounce package frozen peas

¼ cup Chicken Stock (page 252)

2 tablespoons unsalted butter or ghee

Zest of 1 orange, minced

¼ cup chopped fresh mint

1 garlic clove, minced

Celtic sea salt and freshly ground black pepper

Leafy Greens with Red Onion and Bacon

My husband was never a fan of leafy greens until he had this dish. He looked at me and said, "This is the perfect way to get me to eat greens. Salty bacon and sweet onion. I like it." For a man who has never enjoyed leafy greens, that's pretty high praise.

SERVES 4 TO 6
PREPARATION TIME: 20 minutes

4 bacon slices, cut into ½-inch pieces

1 red onion, diced

1 large bunch of Swiss chard, kale, or mustard greens, coarsely chopped

Celtic sea salt and freshly ground black pepper

Cook the bacon in a large skillet over medium heat until crisp, 5 to 7 minutes. Transfer the bacon to a small bowl with a slotted spoon, leaving the drippings in the pan. Add the onion to the pan and sauté until golden brown, about 4 minutes. Add the greens and stir occasionally until wilted, 2 to 3 minutes. Season generously with salt and pepper. Top with the bacon and serve immediately.

Remember, it's important to eat saturated fats with vegetables because many of the vitamins and micronutrients in these foods are fat soluble. This means they can't be absorbed without the presence of fat. So if you eat fruits or vegetables without fat, your body won't be able to assimilate many of the nutrients.

Zucchini Fritters

The key to crisp zucchini fritters is sea salt and an absorbent, clean dish towel. Allowing the shredded zucchini to sit with sea salt for thirty minutes draws out much of the water, and wringing it in a towel ensures that the excess water is removed. It's amazing what a difference this step can make. This is also a great trick when using zucchini in breads and muffins.

SERVES 4
PREPARATION TIME: 50 minutes

FRITTERS

1 pound zucchini, shredded

2 teaspoons Celtic sea salt

2 scallions, finely chopped

¼ cup arrowroot flour

1 tablespoon coconut flour

½ teaspoon freshly ground black pepper

2 large eggs, beaten

1 cup crumbled feta cheese

¼ cup ghee

TOPPINGS

½ cup sour cream

4 lemon wedges

4 chives, minced

1. Toss the zucchini and 1½ teaspoons of the salt in a colander. Set the colander in the sink and let the zucchini drain for 30 minutes. Pour the zucchini out onto a clean dish towel. Wrap the towel around the zucchini and squeeze out as much liquid as you can. Place the zucchini in a large mixing bowl.

2. Preheat the oven to 200°F and adjust the rack to the middle position. Place a cooling rack on top of a baking sheet and set it next to the stove.

3. Add the scallions, arrowroot flour, coconut flour, black pepper, and remaining ½ teaspoon salt to the zucchini and toss well. Add the eggs and feta and stir until incorporated.

4. Heat a large skillet over medium heat for 2 minutes. Add 2 tablespoons of the ghee and swirl to coat. Spoon ¼ cup of the batter into the pan for each fritter and push down gently on the batter to flatten. You can fit 6 or 7 fritters in the pan at once. Fry until the bottoms of the fritters are golden brown, 2 to 3 minutes. Using a spatula, flip the fritters and fry the other side until golden brown, another 2 to 3 minutes. Place the fritters on the prepared baking sheet. Keep warm in the oven while you repeat with the remaining batter.

5. Serve the fritters with a dollop of sour cream, a spritz of lemon juice, and a sprinkling of chives.

PALEO/DAIRY-FREE ADAPTATION: Omit the cheese and use only 1 egg to make the fritters. Use lard or tallow in place of the ghee. Use Savory Cashew "Cheese" (page 264) in place of the sour cream.

Bacon, Mushroom, and Chard "Rice" Bowl

Sometimes you just want something with familiar flavors. Bacon, mushrooms, and cheese are three of my favorite comfort foods. You can change up this recipe by using other greens, adding ground beef, or using a different cheese.

SERVES 4

PREPARATION TIME: 20 minutes

8 bacon slices, chopped

8 ounces white mushrooms, sliced

2 small yellow onions, chopped

1 bunch of Swiss chard, thick stems removed, chopped

3 garlic cloves, chopped

1 recipe "Riced" Cauliflower (page 263)

Celtic sea salt

1 cup shredded Cheddar cheese

1. Heat a large skillet over medium heat. Add the bacon and fry until the fat starts to melt, about 5 minutes. Add the mushrooms and sauté for 5 to 7 minutes, until the bacon is crispy and the mushrooms lose their moisture and begin to caramelize. Transfer the mushrooms and bacon to a bowl with a slotted spoon and cover to keep warm.

2. Add the onions and chard to the bacon fat left in the skillet and sauté for 5 minutes, until soft. Add the garlic and stir for about 1 minute, until fragrant. Add the cauliflower "rice" and stir for about 1 minute. Season to taste with salt.

3. Spoon the "rice" into bowls and sprinkle with the bacon, mushrooms, and cheese.

PALEO/DAIRY-FREE ADAPTATION: Omit the cheese.

NOTE: You can also make this into a casserole—it's great for potlucks! Add ½ cup sour cream or Savory Cashew "Cheese" (page 264) to the cauliflower mixture, pour into an 8 x 8-inch baking dish, top with the bacon-mushroom mixture and an additional ½ cup cheese, and bake at 350°F for about 20 minutes, or until golden brown on top.

Grain-Free Stuffing

If you like stuffing, then this dish needs to make a showing at your Thanksgiving feast. This is one of the best-loved savory recipes on my blog. Many readers have written to tell me that their guests raved over the flavors and had no idea it was grain free. To make things easier, you can prepare the biscuits a few weeks ahead of time, freeze them, and then set them out to thaw and dry before putting the stuffing together.

1. Preheat the oven to 350°F and adjust the rack to the middle position. Butter an 11 x 7-inch baking dish.

2. Melt the butter in a large skillet over medium heat. Add the onions and stir occasionally until golden brown and caramelized, about 20 minutes. Add the sage and stir for about 30 seconds, until fragrant. Remove the skillet from the heat and add the biscuit pieces to the onion mixture.

3. In a small bowl, whisk the egg, heavy cream, and chicken stock and pour it over the biscuit mixture. Season with the salt and pepper and stir until incorporated. Pour the stuffing into the prepared baking dish and bake for 30 to 40 minutes, until golden brown.

PALEO/DAIRY-FREE ADAPTATION: Use coconut oil in place of the butter. Use canned coconut milk in place of the heavy cream.

SERVES 8

PREPARATION TIME: 1 hour
(most of this is baking time)

3 tablespoons unsalted butter, plus more for the dish

2 large yellow onions, chopped

15 fresh sage leaves, chopped

12 stale Grain-Free Biscuits (page 31), broken into small pieces

1 large egg

¼ cup heavy cream

¼ cup Chicken Stock (page 252)

1 teaspoon coarse Celtic sea salt

⅛ teaspoon freshly ground black pepper

Roasted Red Onions

It may seem odd to serve onions as a side dish, but these little purple beauties develop a mellow sweetness when roasted and are always a huge hit with the family. I usually pair them with roasted chicken or hamburgers.

1. Preheat the oven to 400°F and adjust the rack to the middle position.

2. Toss the onions with the ghee and spread them evenly on a baking sheet. Season generously with salt and pepper. Roast for 15 minutes, stir, and roast for an additional 15 minutes, until the onions begin to caramelize (they will turn golden brown on the edges). Serve immediately.

PALEO/DAIRY-FREE ADAPTATION: Use tallow or lard in place of the ghee.

NOTE: Make a double batch and add to scrambled eggs or a frittata for breakfast.

SERVES 4 TO 5
PREPARATION TIME: 35 minutes

3 red onions, cut into ½-inch wedges

3 tablespoons ghee, melted

Celtic sea salt and freshly ground black pepper

Cauliflower "Fried Rice"

I've served this to numerous friends and they are always surprised at how great it tastes. I'm not trying to fool anyone into thinking this is rice, but it sure comes close. This makes a fabulous accompaniment to any stir-fry.

SERVES 6

PREPARATION TIME: 50 minutes

2 heads of cauliflower,
cut into bite-size pieces

1 cup frozen peas, thawed

2 carrots, diced

3 tablespoons coconut oil

5 tablespoons fermented tamari
sauce, plus more to taste

3 large eggs

4 scallions, white and green parts,
chopped

1. Place half the cauliflower in the bowl of a food processor. Pulse for 12 to 15 one-second pulses, or until the cauliflower is about the size of grains of rice. Transfer to a bowl and repeat with the rest of the cauliflower.

2. Place the peas and carrots in a small saucepan and cover with water. Bring to a simmer over medium heat and cook until tender, 8 to 10 minutes. Drain.

3. Heat a large skillet over medium heat for 2 minutes. Add the coconut oil and swirl to coat. Add the cauliflower and tamari and cook, stirring occasionally, until the cauliflower is hot and coated with the tamari, about 3 minutes. Move the cauliflower to the outside edge of the pan to make a space for the eggs. Crack the eggs into the center of the pan and scramble them there, then stir them into the cauliflower. Add the peas, carrots, and scallions and cook, stirring, for about 2 minutes, until all the ingredients are incorporated and hot. Season to taste with a bit more tamari if needed. Serve immediately.

PALEO/DAIRY-FREE ADAPTATION: Use coconut aminos in place of the tamari.

NOTE: To turn this recipe into a main dish, mix 1 pound ground chicken with 2 tablespoons fermented tamari sauce and marinate for 30 minutes in the fridge. Cook the meat thoroughly in a skillet, breaking it into small pieces with the back of a spoon, then mix it in with the cauliflower before adding the eggs.

Sweet Potato Casserole

Most Thanksgiving tables feature a sweet potato casserole. I enjoy the subtle, creamy sweetness combined with the crunchy, sweet-salty pecan topping. This version isn't too sweet, but you can add more honey if you want. Use either cream or coconut milk, depending on your dietary needs. You can make the potato mixture two days ahead of time and store it in the refrigerator before adding the topping and baking it.

SERVES 8
PREPARATION TIME: 35 minutes

SWEET POTATOES

3 cups mashed baked sweet potatoes (3 or 4 large potatoes; see Note)

¼ cup raw honey

2 large eggs, beaten

8 tablespoons (1 stick) unsalted butter, melted

½ cup heavy cream

1½ teaspoons Pure Vanilla Extract (page 274)

¼ teaspoon Celtic sea salt

TOPPING

1 cup almond flour

2 tablespoons coconut flour

2 tablespoons raw honey

⅛ teaspoon Celtic sea salt

4 tablespoons (½ stick) unsalted butter, melted

1 cup chopped pecans

1. Preheat the oven to 350°F and adjust the rack to the middle position.

2. Combine all the sweet potato ingredients thoroughly in a large bowl and spread the mixture evenly in an 11 x 7-inch baking dish.

3. To make the topping, combine the almond flour, coconut flour, honey, salt, and butter in a medium bowl. Stir in the pecans. Sprinkle the topping evenly over the sweet potatoes and bake for 20 minutes, until golden brown.

PALEO/DAIRY-FREE ADAPTATION: For the potatoes, use 6 tablespoons coconut oil in place of the butter and canned coconut milk instead of the heavy cream. For the topping, use 3 tablespoons coconut oil in place of the butter.

NOTE: Bake the sweet potatoes at 400°F for 45 minutes, or until soft. Remove the skins when the potatoes have cooled to room temperature, and mash until smooth.

Sautéed Kale with Raisins and Walnuts

My mom taught me long ago that whenever you're adding raisins to a dish, always plump them in liquid first. Letting the raisins sit in a warm liquid such as orange juice or rum for about 15 minutes transforms the little fruits into marvelous sweet jewels.

1. Place the orange juice and raisins in a small saucepan and bring to a low simmer. Remove from the heat and let sit for 15 minutes. Drain.

2. Melt the ghee in a large sauté pan over medium heat. Add the garlic and cook until fragrant, about 1 minute. Add the kale and sauté until just wilted and bright green, 3 to 4 minutes. Season with salt and pepper and sprinkle with the walnuts and raisins. Serve immediately.

PALEO/DAIRY-FREE ADAPTATION: Use coconut oil in place of the ghee.

SERVES 4
PREPARATION TIME: 25 minutes

½ cup orange juice

¼ cup raisins

2 tablespoons ghee

2 garlic cloves, minced

1 bunch of kale, thick stems removed, chopped

¼ teaspoon Celtic sea salt

⅛ teaspoon freshly ground black pepper

¼ cup walnuts

Roasted Vegetables with Caramelized Onion Mayonnaise

My friend Molly from Apricot Lane Farms makes a version of this dish that is simply delicious. Freshly picked vegetables are tossed in ghee and roasted until golden and sweet, then topped with homemade caramelized onion mayonnaise made from eggs freshly laid by the hens out in the pasture. We ate this dish along with grass-fed beef hamburgers one night on Molly's patio under the stars. It's a simple memory, but one I hold dear. It's "farm to table" in a nutshell. You don't have to have fancy ingredients to make a dynamite dish.

SERVES 4
PREPARATION TIME: 20 minutes

1 head of broccoli, cut into bite-size pieces

2 red, yellow, or orange bell peppers, cut into bite-size pieces

1 head of cauliflower, cut into bite-size pieces

¼ cup ghee, melted

Celtic sea salt

Caramelized Onion Mayonnaise (recipe follows)

1. Preheat the oven to 400°F and adjust the rack to the middle position.

2. In a large bowl, toss the vegetables with the ghee and season with salt. Spread the vegetables evenly on a baking sheet. Roast for 10 minutes, stir, and roast for 10 minutes more, or until golden brown on the edges. Serve with caramelized onion mayonnaise.

PALEO/DAIRY-FREE ADAPTATION: Use lard or tallow in place of the ghee.

Caramelized Onion Mayonnaise

This mayonnaise is wonderful on grilled meats or as a dip for raw vegetables.

1. Place the onion and olive oil in a large sauté pan over medium-low heat. Sauté, stirring occasionally, until the onion softens and turns golden brown, 20 to 25 minutes.

2. To make the mayonnaise, combine the yolks, Dijon, lemon juice, and salt in a food processor or blender and blend for 30 seconds. With the processor running, very slowly add the light olive oil (it should take about 1 minute to add all the oil). Pour the mayonnaise into a bowl, stir in the onion, and season to taste with salt. Store leftover mayonnaise in an airtight container for up to 5 days.

MAKES 1 CUP
PREPARATION TIME: 30 minutes

ONION

1 yellow onion, diced

2 tablespoons extra-virgin olive oil

MAYONNAISE

2 large egg yolks

½ teaspoon Dijon mustard

Juice of 1 lemon

½ teaspoon Celtic sea salt, plus more to taste

¾ cup light olive oil

Green Bean Casserole

This is a can-free casserole. I think we've all had green bean casserole at one time or another. Traditionally, it's prepared with canned mushroom soup and canned fried onions, both of which contain many processed ingredients. This is a healthier, lighter version using roasted red onions for the crispy topping and a quick, homemade cream of mushroom soup.

SERVES 8 TO 10
PREPARATION TIME: 50 minutes

2 red onions, thinly sliced

2 tablespoons ghee, melted

Celtic sea salt and freshly ground black pepper

2 pounds green beans, trimmed and halved

3 tablespoons unsalted butter

1 pound white mushrooms, sliced

2 tablespoons arrowroot flour

1½ cups Chicken Stock (page 252)

1½ cups heavy cream

1. Preheat the oven to 425°F and adjust the rack to the middle position.

2. In a large bowl, toss together the red onions and ghee and season generously with salt and pepper. Spread the onions on a large baking sheet and roast for 5 minutes. Using a spatula, stir the onions and roast for another 10 minutes, or until they lose most of their moisture and begin to turn golden brown. Set the onions aside and reduce the oven heat to 375°F.

3. Meanwhile, bring a large pot of water to a boil over medium-high heat. Add the green beans and boil for 6 minutes, or until crisp-tender. Drain and rinse with cold water to stop the cooking process. Set aside.

4. Melt the butter in a large skillet over medium heat. When the foaming subsides, add the mushrooms and season generously with salt and pepper. Sauté until the mushrooms have released their moisture and the edges begin to turn golden brown, about 10 minutes. Add the arrowroot flour and stir constantly until incorporated, about 1 minute. Slowly pour in the chicken stock and then the cream, whisking constantly to avoid creating lumps. Reduce the heat to low and simmer until the sauce thickens, 6 to 8 minutes.

5. Add the green beans to the mushroom mixture and toss gently to combine. Season to taste with salt. Pour the mixture into a 13 x 9-inch baking dish. Spread the onions in an even layer on top and bake until bubbling, 20 to 25 minutes.

PALEO/DAIRY-FREE ADAPTATION: Use coconut oil in place of the ghee and butter. Substitute 1 cup almond milk and ½ cup coconut milk for the cream.

Honey-Roasted Parsnips and Beets

It's incredible how a simple vegetable can take on such sweetness and flavor when combined with ghee, honey, and a lot of heat. This is the simplest of recipes, but your guests will be coming back for seconds.

1. Preheat the oven to 400°F and adjust the rack to the middle position.

2. In a large bowl, toss the parsnips and beets with the ghee, then spread them evenly on a baking sheet. Roast for 10 minutes. Pour the honey over the vegetables and toss carefully. Roast for 15 to 20 minutes more, or until the edges are golden brown. Splash with coconut vinegar, toss, and serve.

PALEO/DAIRY-FREE ADAPTATION: Substitute coconut oil for the ghee.

SERVES 4

PREPARATION TIME: 30 minutes

1 pound parsnips, peeled and cut into ¼-inch coins

1 pound beets, peeled and cut into ¼-inch slices

¼ cup ghee or palm shortening, melted

¼ cup raw honey

1 tablespoon coconut vinegar

It's important to use ghee instead of butter or olive oil when roasting. Butter and olive oil have a lower smoking point (the point at which the oil smokes and oxidizes, creating free radicals). Ghee is butter with the milk solids removed, so it can withstand very high temperatures without oxidizing. See the really easy recipe for homemade ghee on page 255.

Creamed Cauliflower

Creamed cauliflower makes a nice substitute for mashed potatoes when you want the rich creaminess without all the carbs. You can add mix-ins such as bacon, scallions, or herbs. I also like to pour it into a baking dish, top it with grated Cheddar, and bake it. And don't worry if the cauliflower head lends a little more or less than 6 cups, since this is a very forgiving recipe and will turn out just fine if you alter the ingredients a bit.

SERVES 4

PREPARATION TIME: 25 minutes

1 large head of cauliflower, cut into bite-size pieces (about 6 cups)

8 tablespoons (1 stick) unsalted butter

2 tablespoons whole milk

½ teaspoon Celtic sea salt

⅛ teaspoon freshly ground black pepper

1. Place the cauliflower in a large pot and add water to cover by 1 inch. Bring the water to a boil over medium-high heat, then turn the heat to medium-low and simmer until the cauliflower is tender, about 15 minutes. Drain.

2. Pour the cauliflower into the bowl of a food processor or blender. Add the butter, milk, salt, and pepper and blend until smooth. Serve.

PALEO/DAIRY-FREE ADAPTATION: Use 2 tablespoons olive oil in place of the butter. Use almond milk in place of the whole milk. Add ½ cup Savory Cashew "Cheese" (page 264) to the mixture.

Main Dishes

Main dishes make up the bulk of most family food budgets and without careful watch, their allotment can be blown quickly. Many of us want to make healthy changes to our diets, but we need help obtaining grain-free foods without breaking the bank. I've spent many years finding ways to cut costs to make grain-free living more affordable for my family. Here are some of my top tips.

Buy food, not packaging. Why pay for cardboard and plastic when that money could go toward food? Packaging costs money, so when possible, buy foods without it.

Buy in season. It seems like an obvious thing to say, but how many of us have succumbed to the bright pink raspberries at the grocery store in December? Buying in season not only ensures you get the biggest bang for your buck, it also means your produce will taste as it should—ripe and full of flavor.

Order pantry staples online. Almond flour, coconut flour, raw honey, and so on are usually more affordable at online stores such as Amazon and Azure Standard. Sometimes you have to buy a few packages to receive a good discount, so I usually order with a few of my friends. Then we split the order and the shipping costs.

Grow your own herbs. A small package of fresh mint can cost $2, but you could pay the same price for a mint plant at your local gardening store (and mint is really easy to grow). I have a few pots and each year I grow basil, oregano, thyme, parsley, mint, and cilantro, which gives me fresh herbs for about six months of the year. If you use herbs often in your cooking, growing your own can save you quite a bit of money. You can also dry the herbs and store them in jars to use in the winter. To dry herbs, simply pick them, lay them on a baking sheet, and leave them out at room temperature for three or four days, until dry and crumbly. Crumble the leaves and store in an airtight container.

Become a member of a CSA or co-op. Get a box of fresh, all-organic produce from a local grower for a fraction of what you'd pay at the store. Check www.localharvest.com for a CSA (community-supported agriculture) in your area. A produce box also exposes me to vegetables that I might not otherwise buy. My favorite way to prepare some of those mystery vegetables is roasting, which brings out the sweetness—a surefire way to get your family to eat veggies, too.

Buy your meat straight from the farm. Organic, pastured meats generally cost more. Having said that, we don't have to pay the incredible prices at the major grocery stores. I like to buy meat straight from the farm because then I know exactly where it's coming from—and I save a substantial amount of money.

You may think you won't find the right kind of farm near you, but it's easier than you think. Each time our family has moved, I've wondered where I'll get my meat, and I've always found a reputable farm to purchase from. It might be a few hours away, but I find a friend or two who wants to order and we drive there together and make a day of it. I use the site EatWild.com to find local organic farms.

Buy in bulk. Purchasing foods in bulk generally costs less. Look for bulk bins at the grocery store or bulk items online. For example, many times I've bought twenty-five pounds of Sucanat and split it with friends because it was half the price. Nuts can also be a higher-price item, so buying them in larger quantities can reduce the cost significantly.

Plan your meals. This is one of the best ways to keep your costs low. Make a menu and shopping list each week and buy only what's on the list. I've saved hundreds of dollars following this rule. And if you need help in this area, check out the Deliciously Organic Weekly Meal Plans on our website.

Maple-Glazed Salmon with Spinach and Bell Peppers

This dish combines two of my favorite weeknight meals—salmon and stir-fry. The salmon is roasted and basted so that it's covered with a sticky-sweet maple and tamari glaze. It's served on a bed of vegetables brought together with a sauce highlighted with sherry (one of my favorite ingredients for a great stir-fry). The vegetables and sauce can be prepped the night before or in the morning to save time in the kitchen after a long day.

1. Preheat the oven to 400°F and adjust the rack to the middle position. Oil a 13 x 9-inch baking dish with sesame oil.

2. For the salmon, whisk the sesame oil, maple syrup, and tamari sauce in a small flat dish. Place the salmon in the mixture, turning to coat both sides. Let sit for 10 minutes. Remove the salmon from the marinade and place it on the oiled baking pan.

3. Roast the salmon for 12 minutes, spooning the marinade over the fish every 5 minutes.

4. Meanwhile, bring the remaining marinade to a simmer in a small saucepan over medium-low heat and simmer for 5 minutes.

5. Whisk all the sauce ingredients in a small bowl.

6. To make the stir-fry, melt the coconut oil in a large sauté pan, swirling to coat. Add the scallions and bell pepper and sauté for 3 to 4 minutes. Move the vegetables to the sides of the pan and add the garlic and ginger in the center, stirring until fragrant, about 1 minute. Stir in the spinach and cook for 3 to 4 minutes, until the spinach has wilted. Pour in the sauce and stir until thickened, about 1 minute. Serve the stir-fry with the salmon and sprinkle with sesame seeds.

PALEO/DAIRY-FREE ADAPTATION: Substitute an equal amount of coconut aminos for the tamari.

SERVES 4

PREPARATION TIME: 30 minutes

SALMON

Sesame oil for baking dish

2 teaspoons toasted sesame oil

¼ cup maple syrup

¼ cup fermented tamari sauce

1 pound wild salmon fillet, cut into 4 pieces

SAUCE

3 tablespoons dry sherry

¼ cup Chicken Stock (page 252)

2 tablespoons fermented tamari sauce

½ teaspoon toasted sesame oil

2 teaspoons arrowroot flour

1 teaspoon maple syrup

STIR-FRY

2 tablespoons coconut oil

8 scallions, cut into 1-inch pieces

2 red bell peppers, cut into bite-size pieces

2 garlic cloves, chopped

1 tablespoon minced fresh ginger

6 cups baby spinach

2 tablespoons sesame seeds

Eggplant and Zucchini Lasagna

Roasted zucchini and eggplant make a nice substitution for noodles. The key is to salt the vegetables to help draw out the moisture (we don't want a watery casserole!) and then roast them to bring out the sweetness. For a vegetarian option, you can omit the ground beef.

SERVES 6

PREPARATION TIME: 1 hour

VEGETABLES

5 medium zucchini, cut lengthwise into ¼-inch-thick slices

2 eggplants, peeled and cut lengthwise into ¼-inch-thick slices

Celtic sea salt

¼ cup ghee, melted

TOMATO-MEAT SAUCE

2 garlic cloves, minced

2 tablespoons extra-virgin olive oil

2 teaspoons dried Italian seasoning

One 24-ounce jar crushed tomatoes

1 teaspoon Celtic sea salt

1½ pounds grass-fed ground beef

RICOTTA FILLING

10 ounces ricotta cheese

1 teaspoon dried Italian seasoning

2 large eggs, beaten

TOPPING

½ cup grated mozzarella cheese

1. Preheat the oven to 425°F and adjust the rack to the middle position.

2. Place the zucchini and eggplant slices on 2 large rimmed baking sheets and sprinkle both sides with salt. Let sit for 20 minutes. Pat the slices dry with a paper towel or dish towel and brush with melted ghee. Roast for 15 minutes, or until the vegetables begin to shrivel a bit and the edges are just turning golden brown. Reduce the heat to 400°F.

3. Meanwhile, to make the tomato-meat sauce, combine the garlic, olive oil, and Italian seasoning in a large saucepan over medium heat. Cook until the garlic begins to sizzle and is fragrant, about 1 minute. Add the tomatoes and salt and simmer the sauce for 10 minutes. Add the ground beef and cook, breaking the beef apart with the back of a wooden spoon, until cooked through, 8 to 10 minutes.

4. For the filling, stir the ricotta, Italian seasoning, and eggs together in a small bowl.

5. Spoon a few tablespoons of the sauce into an 11 x 7-inch baking dish and spread evenly to coat the bottom of the dish. Top with half of the zucchini and eggplant slices (they will overlap). Spread half of the ricotta mixture on top, followed by half the remaining sauce. Repeat with the remaining ingredients and top with the mozzarella. Bake for 25 to 30 minutes, until the lasagna is bubbling and the cheese is golden brown on top.

PALEO/DAIRY-FREE ADAPTATION: Use coconut oil in place of the ghee. Use Savory Cashew "Cheese" (page 264) in place of the ricotta. Omit the mozzarella.

Creamy Chicken, Vegetable, and Tomato Soup

I have a secret for all my soups: Sweat the vegetables. It's amazing how you can transform the flavor of a soup with such a simple technique. I usually chop up some carrots, onions, celery, and garlic and throw them into a large pot with a few tablespoons of melted butter. (Remember, you want to eat your vegetables with a healthy amount of fat so your body can assimilate the nutrients properly.) I put on the lid, turn the heat as low as it will go, and leave it to cook for 30 minutes. This creates a smooth, buttery base for soups and stews.

1. Melt the butter in a large soup pot or Dutch oven. Add the carrots, leek, celery, and garlic. Stir, cover the pot, and reduce the heat to low. Cook for 30 minutes.

2. Add the mushrooms and 1 teaspoon of the salt to the pot. Stir and cook for 10 minutes, or until the mushrooms have released their moisture. Stir in the Italian seasoning and cook for 1 minute.

3. Add the stock, chicken, tomatoes, and remaining 1 teaspoon salt. Bring to a simmer and cook until the chicken is cooked through, about 20 minutes. Remove the chicken from the pot, cut it into bite size pieces, and add it back to the soup. Stir in the cream and season to taste. Serve.

PALEO/DAIRY-FREE ADAPTATION: Use lard or tallow in place of the butter. Use coconut milk in place of the cream.

SERVES 6
PREPARATION TIME: 55 minutes

4 tablespoons (½ stick) unsalted butter

4 large carrots, chopped

1 large leek, trimmed and chopped

2 celery stalks, chopped

4 garlic cloves, minced

8 ounces mushrooms, sliced

2 teaspoons Celtic sea salt, plus more to taste

2 teaspoons dried Italian seasoning

1 quart Chicken Stock (page 252)

3 boneless, skinless chicken breasts

One 24-ounce jar crushed tomatoes

½ cup heavy cream

Grilled Asian Pork Chops with Cremini Mushrooms and Scallions

It's quite the treat to find an organic, pastured piece of pork, so when we do, we do very little to the meat so we can enjoy the "pigness of the pig," as Joel Salatin would say. I can't find organic, pastured pork in my area, so I order from Tendergrass Farms, an organization of farm partners that makes mail-order meat a cinch.

SERVES 4

PREPARATION TIME: 1 hour 20 minutes (most of this is marinating time)

PORK CHOPS

½ cup fermented tamari sauce

¼ cup dry sherry

¼ cup grated fresh ginger

4 garlic cloves, minced

4 pork loin chops

MUSHROOMS AND SCALLIONS

1 tablespoon coconut oil

1 pound cremini mushrooms, sliced

10 scallions, white and green parts, chopped

1. Whisk the tamari sauce, sherry, ginger, and garlic in a small bowl. Place the pork chops in a baking dish and pour half the marinade on top.

2. Heat the remaining marinade in a small saucepan over medium heat. Place the mushrooms in a medium bowl and pour the hot marinade on top. Let the pork chops and mushrooms marinate for 1 hour at room temperature.

3. Preheat the grill on medium heat and grill the pork chops on both sides until cooked through, about 4 minutes per side. If you need to cook indoors, you can heat the broiler on high and broil the pork chops for 3 to 4 minutes per side, until cooked through. Place the chops on a serving dish and tent with foil to let rest.

4. Heat the coconut oil in a medium sauté pan over medium heat, swirling to coat. Drain the mushrooms, add them to the pan, and cook until they release their juices, 5 to 7 minutes. Stir in the scallions and cook until hot, about 1 minute. Serve the pork chops with scallions and mushrooms spooned on top.

PALEO/DAIRY-FREE ADAPTATION: Use coconut aminos in place of the tamari.

General Tso's Chicken

I love a good stir-fry. Although the ingredient list is a bit longer than most recipes, the meat can be marinated, the vegetables chopped, and the sauces mixed early in the day so the meal can be cooked on a hot skillet in a flash. I like to serve this dish with Cauliflower "Fried Rice" (page 132).

1. To make the chicken marinade, in a medium bowl, whisk together the egg, arrowroot flour, tamari sauce, ginger, and sherry. Add the chicken and toss to coat. Let the chicken sit for 20 minutes.

2. To make the sauce, in a small bowl, whisk together the arrowroot flour, tamari sauce, chicken stock, sesame oil, ginger, honey, and vinegar.

3. To make the stir-fry, heat a large skillet over medium heat for 2 minutes. Add 2 tablespoons of the coconut oil and swirl to coat. Add half the chicken to the pan, making sure the pieces are in a single layer. Cook, stirring once, until the chicken is no longer pink inside, about 4 minutes. Transfer the cooked chicken to a plate and repeat with the remaining coconut oil and chicken.

4. Place the broccoli in the pan and cook, stirring frequently, about 2 minutes. Add ¼ cup water and quickly put the lid on. Cook for 2 minutes, then remove the lid. Continue to cook the broccoli until the water has evaporated. Move the broccoli to the sides of the pan and add the garlic, ginger, and scallions to the center. Cook and stir until fragrant, about 1 minute. Stir to combine with the broccoli, add the sauce, and cook until the sauce begins to thicken, about 1 minute. Return the chicken to the skillet and toss to incorporate.

PALEO/DAIRY-FREE ADAPTATION: Substitute coconut aminos for the tamari sauce.

SERVES 4

PREPARATION TIME: 50 minutes

CHICKEN

1 large egg

¼ cup arrowroot flour

3 tablespoons fermented tamari sauce

1 teaspoon minced fresh ginger

2 teaspoons dry sherry

1 pound boneless, skinless chicken breasts, cut into bite-size pieces

SAUCE

1 tablespoon arrowroot flour

1 tablespoon fermented tamari sauce

¼ cup Chicken Stock (page 252)

1 teaspoon toasted sesame oil

1 teaspoon grated fresh ginger

1 tablespoon raw honey (I use clover)

1 tablespoon rice vinegar

STIR FRY

¼ cup coconut oil

1 head of broccoli, cut into bite-size pieces

2 garlic cloves, minced

1 tablespoon minced fresh ginger

1 bunch of scallions, white and green parts, chopped

Beef Taco Bowl

If you come to my house during the week, you'll probably find me having a beef taco-less bowl for lunch. I make a large batch on the weekends and reheat it throughout the week. Vegetables, spices, pastured ground beef, and spicy salsa make for a nutritious and delightful midday meal.

SERVES 4 TO 6

PREPARATION TIME: 45 minutes

FILLING

2 tablespoons coconut oil

1 yellow onion, chopped

2 carrots, chopped

1 red, orange, or yellow bell pepper, chopped

1 pound grass-fed ground beef

2 garlic cloves, minced

2 teaspoons ground cumin

1 teaspoon Celtic sea salt, plus more to taste

TOPPINGS

1 cup salsa

1 avocado, diced

1 cup shredded Cheddar cheese (optional)

¼ cup sour cream (optional)

¼ cup minced fresh cilantro

1 lime, quartered

1. Place the coconut oil in a large skillet over medium heat. Swirl to coat the pan. Add the onion, carrots, and bell pepper and sauté until softened and just turning golden brown on the edges, 5 to 8 minutes.

2. Add the ground beef and cook, stirring frequently and breaking up the meat with the back of a spoon until browned, 6 to 8 minutes. Move the meat mixture to the sides of the pan and sprinkle the garlic, cumin, and salt in the center. Stir the spices in the center until fragrant, about 1 minute. Combine the spices with the meat mixture. Taste and add more salt if needed. Remove the skillet from the heat.

3. Serve the meat in a bowl topped with salsa, avocado, cheese, sour cream, cilantro, and a squeeze of lime juice.

Bunless Turkey-Spinach Burgers with Sun-Dried Tomato Pesto

My family isn't a huge fan of spinach, but we all give a thumbs-up for these burgers. Spinach in a turkey burger is a clever way to add a few extra nutrients—and it's a great-tasting combination, too. I prefer to serve bunless burgers on big pieces of iceberg lettuce. This crunchy lettuce is a winner for grain-free burgers as it's big enough to wrap around the meat and hearty enough not to fall apart or let any juices drip onto your lap.

SERVES 4

PREPARATION TIME: 35 minutes

SUN-DRIED TOMATO PESTO

2 cups oil-packed sun-dried tomatoes, drained

1 cup grated Pecorino Romano cheese

1 cup walnuts

2 garlic cloves

½ cup extra-virgin olive oil

Celtic sea salt

TURKEY-SPINACH BURGERS

5 ounces spinach

1 pound ground turkey

1 teaspoon dried Italian seasoning

½ teaspoon garlic powder

½ teaspoon Celtic sea salt

TO SERVE

4 large iceberg lettuce leaves

4 thick slices fresh mozzarella cheese

1. Place the sun-dried tomatoes, Pecorino Romano cheese, walnuts, and garlic in the bowl of a food processor. Process until blended. With the processor running, slowly add the olive oil. Season to taste with salt.

2. Bring a medium saucepan of water to a boil over medium-high heat. Add the spinach and cook for 1 minute, until bright green and limp. Drain. When the spinach is cool enough to handle, squeeze out the water and chop the spinach into small pieces.

3. Preheat a grill on medium. In a large bowl, mix the ground turkey, Italian seasoning, garlic powder, spinach, and salt until blended. (Don't mix the meat too long or it will become tough when cooked.) Divide the meat into 4 portions and flatten each into a ¾-inch-thick patty. Gently press down the center of each patty to create a slight depression, about ½ inch in diameter. Grill to the desired doneness, 3 to 4 minutes per side.

4. To serve, place a turkey burger on top of a lettuce leaf. Top the burgers with a smear of pesto and a slice of mozzarella cheese.

PALEO/DAIRY-FREE ADAPTATION: Substitute 1 tablespoon nutritional yeast for the Pecorino Romano. Omit the mozzarella.

NOTE: You will have leftover pesto after making this recipe. You can dollop it over roasted meats or sautéed vegetables or freeze it in an airtight container for up to 3 months.

Southwestern Stuffed Bell Peppers

Stuffed bell peppers have regained their place at the table in our home. The Southwest flavors of cumin, chiles, and Monterey Jack cheese add zesty flavor. In place of brown rice, I used "riced" cauliflower. (I didn't tell the family there was cauliflower in the dish and no one knew!) It's a dinner that can be prepared ahead of time, stored in the fridge, and popped in the oven on a busy evening. It's a simple, nourishing, and vibrant one-dish meal.

Depending on the size of the peppers, you might have a bit of filling left over. If so, put the filling in a small oven-proof bowl and bake alongside the peppers. It makes a great lunch the next day!

SERVES 4 TO 6

PREPARATION TIME: 50 minutes

2 tablespoons coconut oil

6 scallions, cut into ¼-inch slices, white and green parts separated

1 pound grass-fed ground beef

1½ teaspoons ground cumin

2 garlic cloves, minced

3 cups "Riced" Cauliflower (page 263)

One 4.5-ounce can chopped green chiles

2 cups shredded Monterey Jack cheese

½ teaspoon Celtic sea salt

4 large red, yellow, or orange bell peppers, cut in half lengthwise, stems on, seeds removed

½ cup sour cream

½ cup salsa

1. Preheat the oven to 375°F and adjust the rack to the middle position.

2. Melt the coconut oil in a large skillet over medium heat. Add the scallion whites, half the scallion greens, and the beef and cook until the meat is no longer pink, 5 to 7 minutes. Move the beef mixture to the sides of the pan and add the cumin and garlic to the center. Stir until fragrant, about 1 minute, then stir into the beef mixture. Add the riced cauliflower, chiles, 1 cup of the cheese, and the salt to the pan and stir until all the ingredients are incorporated.

3. Place the peppers cut side up in a large baking dish. Divide the filling mixture evenly among the peppers. Pour ½ cup hot water in the bottom of the pan and cover the peppers with a sheet of unbleached parchment paper. Top with a piece of foil (this way the foil doesn't touch the food) and press it around the dish to secure it. Bake for 25 minutes. Remove the foil, top each pepper with a bit of sour cream and salsa, and sprinkle on the remaining 1 cup cheese. Bake for 10 minutes, or until the cheese is bubbly and golden brown and the peppers are crisp-tender. Serve.

PALEO/DAIRY-FREE ADAPTATION: Use ½ cup Savory Cashew "Cheese" (page 264) in place of the Monterey Jack. Omit the sour cream.

Slow Cooker Sunday Roast

We buy our pastured, organic beef in bulk once a year from a local farmer. It's a great way to buy nutritious meat at an economical price, but I usually run into the predicament of having some cuts of beef that I just don't know what to do with. This Sunday roast is the perfect recipe for any large cut of meat, and the fact that it cooks in the slow cooker makes it the perfect dinner for a lazy Sunday.

1. Place the butter, honey, wine, tamari, lemon juice, Dijon, hot sauce, salt, pepper, and garlic powder in a medium saucepan over medium heat. Whisk until the butter is melted and the mixture is smooth.

2. Place the roast in a slow cooker and pour the butter mixture on top. Cover and cook for 8 hours on low heat. I love to serve this with Green Beans with Onion and Ham (page 119) and Roasted Red Onions (page 131).

PALEO/DAIRY-FREE ADAPTATION: Use ¼ cup ghee or coconut oil in place of the butter.

SERVES 4 TO 6
PREPARATION TIME: 8 hours

8 tablespoons (1 stick) unsalted butter

½ cup raw honey

½ cup red wine

½ cup fermented tamari sauce or coconut aminos

¼ cup fresh lemon juice

2 teaspoons Dijon mustard

¼ cup hot sauce

2 teaspoons Celtic sea salt

¼ teaspoon freshly ground black pepper

2 teaspoons garlic powder

One 4- to 5-pound grass-fed rump or chuck roast

Chicken Parmesan
with Zucchini Noodles

I prefer to use ghee in place of olive oil in this dish because ghee has a higher smoke point. This way I know the oil won't burn and oxidize while I'm cooking. You'll have leftover spaghetti sauce. You can freeze it for later use.

SERVES 4

PREPARATION TIME: 1 hour 10 minutes

ZUCCHINI NOODLES

2 pounds zucchini, cut into noodles using a noodle slicer, or sliced thin with a vegetable peeler

½ teaspoon Celtic sea salt

2 tablespoons extra-virgin olive oil

MARINARA

1 tablespoon extra-virgin olive oil

2 garlic cloves, minced

One 24-ounce jar crushed tomatoes (I prefer Eden Organic)

½ teaspoon Celtic sea salt

½ teaspoon dried Italian seasoning

CHICKEN

4 boneless, skinless chicken breasts, pounded thin

Celtic sea salt

1 cup almond flour

2 large eggs

2 tablespoons ghee

½ cup grated Pecorino Romano or 4 slices of mozzarella cheese

1. Place the zucchini noodles in a colander and season with salt. Toss, then let sit for 20 minutes to drain. Place a clean dish towel on the counter and pour the zucchini onto the towel. Fold the towel over the zucchini and gently press to dry the noodles.

2. Meanwhile, make the marinara: Heat the olive oil and garlic in a medium saucepan over medium heat. When the garlic begins to sizzle, about 1 minute, add the tomatoes, salt, and Italian seasoning (try to stand back a bit, as the sauce may splatter). Simmer on low for 10 minutes.

3. Set a cooling rack over a large baking sheet. Season the chicken with salt. Place the flour in one flat-bottomed dish and whisk the eggs in another. Heat a large skillet over medium heat for 2 minutes. Add the ghee, melt, and swirl to coat the pan. Dip the chicken into the eggs, then coat both sides with the flour and place in the pan. Cook, without moving, for 4 minutes, or until the bottom is golden brown. Flip the chicken and cook another 4 to 5 minutes, until the other side is golden brown. Transfer the chicken to the prepared baking sheet (this keeps the crust from getting soggy). Top each piece of chicken with some grated Pecorino Romano (or a slice of mozzarella).

4. Preheat the broiler to high.

5. Place the chicken under the broiler and broil until the cheese is melted, about 2 minutes. Watch carefully so that it doesn't burn!

6. Wipe the empty skillet with paper towels, pour in 2 tablespoons olive oil, and heat over medium heat. Add the zucchini noodles and toss with tongs until hot, about 2 minutes.

7. Serve the chicken with the marinara and zucchini noodles.

PALEO/DAIRY-FREE ADAPTATION: Use lard or tallow in place of the ghee. Omit the cheese.

NOTE: I use Pecorino Romano in place of Parmesan because it's more economical and has a nice salty bite.

Bacon-Wrapped Meat Loaf

For most people, liver is at the bottom of the list of desired foods, but it's actually the most nutrient-dense of all foods! It has vitamins A and B and iron, so it's a great addition to the diet. I made this meat loaf for the family one night and didn't mention the added liver. Everyone ate it and complimented the food. After the meal, I told them that I included liver in the meat loaf. They all agreed that they couldn't taste it and it was a great way to add some extra nutrients. It's important to chop the vegetables finely, so I blitz them a few times in the food processor to save time. I usually serve this with creamed cauliflower and a salad.

SERVES 8

PREPARATION TIME: 2 hours
(most of this is baking time)

4 tablespoons (½ stick) unsalted butter

1 carrot, finely chopped

1 celery stalk, finely chopped

1 red bell pepper, finely chopped

2 teaspoons Celtic sea salt

1 tablespoon dried thyme

2 large eggs, gently beaten

¼ pound (4 ounces) beef liver

2 pounds grass-fed ground beef

½ cup almond flour

6 bacon slices

2 tablespoons maple syrup

1. Preheat the oven to 350°F and adjust the rack to the middle position.

2. Heat the butter over medium heat in a large skillet. Add the carrot, celery, and bell pepper and sauté for 5 to 7 minutes, until soft. Move the vegetables to the sides of the pan and add the salt and thyme in the center. Stir until fragrant, about 30 seconds, then stir the seasonings into the vegetables. Remove the pan from the heat and let the mixture cool for about 10 minutes.

3. Place the eggs and liver in the bowl of a food processor or blender and blend until smooth. Place the ground beef, almond flour, and liver mixture in a large bowl. Add the cooled vegetables and stir until combined. Pour the mixture into a 9 x 11-inch baking dish and form into a large loaf. Arrange the bacon in a crisscross pattern on top and use a pastry brush to brush the top with maple syrup. Pour ¾ cup water in the bottom of the pan. (This keeps the meat loaf moist.) Bake for 1½ hours, or until golden brown. Let the meat loaf rest for 10 minutes before serving.

PALEO/DAIRY-FREE ADAPTATION: Use 3 tablespoons coconut oil in place of the butter.

Sautéed Chicken with Squash and Carrot Ribbons

Remember that it's best to buy pastured, organic chicken, since it's higher in omega-3 fatty acids (the good oils found in salmon) than its conventional counterpart. If the chicken breasts are thick, either cut them in half horizontally or pound them with a meat pounder to ensure even cooking.

SERVES 4

PREPARATION TIME: 20 minutes

1 pound yellow squash

1 pound carrots

¼ cup ghee

4 boneless, skinless chicken breasts, pounded thin

1 teaspoon Celtic sea salt

½ cup chopped fresh basil leaves

Juice of 1 lemon

¼ cup chopped fresh flat-leaf parsley

1. Using a vegetable peeler, cut the squash and carrots into ribbons. Place them in a large bowl.

2. Heat a large skillet over medium-high heat for 1 minute. Add 2 tablespoons of the ghee, let it melt, and swirl to coat the pan. Season both sides of the chicken with ½ teaspoon of the salt and place the chicken in the pan. Cook for 4 minutes, until the bottom is just turning golden brown. Using tongs, flip the chicken and cook 3 to 4 minutes more, until cooked through. Set the chicken aside on a plate.

3. Melt the remaining 2 tablespoons ghee in the pan and swirl to coat. Add the squash and carrots and cook for 2 or 3 minutes, or until just soft, tossing occasionally. Remove from the heat, add the basil, lemon juice, and remaining ½ teaspoon salt, and toss.

4. Serve the chicken with the vegetable ribbons and garnish with parsley.

PALEO/DAIRY-FREE ADAPTATION: Use coconut oil in place of the ghee.

Grilled Rib Eye with Asparagus

This is my all-time favorite marinade—my mom passed it on to me many years ago. There's just something about the combination of the tamari, red wine vinegar, garlic, and pepper that brings out the best flavors of a nice piece of beef. This recipe can also be used with flank, sirloin, or tenderloin.

1. Place the steaks in a shallow dish. Whisk together the tamari sauce, vinegar, and olive oil and pour over the steak. Season with the garlic and black pepper. Cover the dish tightly and place in the refrigerator. Marinate for 2 hours.

2. Toss the asparagus with the ghee and season with salt.

3. Preheat the grill to medium-high and grill the steak to the desired doneness. When the steak is done, place it on a cutting board and tent it with foil. Let the meat rest for 5 minutes, then slice it thin, against the grain. While the meat is resting, grill the asparagus until it's just turning golden brown on the edges, 2 to 3 minutes. Serve.

PALEO/DAIRY-FREE ADAPTATION: Use coconut aminos in place of the tamari. Use palm shortening in place of the ghee.

SERVES 4

PREPARATION TIME: 2 hours 45 minutes

4 rib-eye steaks, about 1½ inches thick

3 tablespoons fermented tamari sauce

2 tablespoons red wine vinegar

¼ cup olive oil

2 teaspoons garlic powder

½ teaspoon freshly ground black pepper

1 pound asparagus

1 tablespoon ghee, melted

Celtic sea salt

Creamy Chicken and Mushroom Pot Pie

Pot pie is comfort and warmth; it just feels like home. A simple filling of chicken, mushrooms, onions, and cream is topped with buttery biscuits. My grain-free version is less complicated than many grain-filled recipes I've made in the past and every bit as pleasing.

SERVES 6

PREPARATION TIME: 1 hour 40 minutes

FILLING

3 bone-in, skin-on chicken breasts

1½ teaspoons Celtic sea salt, plus more for the chicken

Freshly ground black pepper

2 tablespoons extra-virgin olive oil

1 yellow onion, minced

5 ounces white mushrooms, sliced

2 garlic cloves, minced

1 teaspoon dried thyme

1 cup heavy cream

BISCUITS

2½ cups almond flour

1 tablespoon coconut flour

½ teaspoon Celtic sea salt

½ teaspoon baking soda

2 teaspoons Grain-Free Baking Powder (page 272)

5 tablespoons cold unsalted butter, cut into tablespoons

¼ cup coconut milk

1. Preheat the oven to 375°F and adjust the rack to the middle position. Season the chicken with salt and pepper to taste and roast for 35 to 40 minutes, or until cooked through. Set the chicken aside to cool for 10 minutes, then shred the meat (discard the skin and bones). Reduce the heat to 350°F.

2. Heat the olive oil in a large skillet over medium heat. Add the onion and mushrooms and sauté until the mushrooms are soft and have released their juices, 10 to 12 minutes. Move the vegetables to the sides of the pan and add the garlic and thyme in the center of the pan. Stir the garlic and thyme until they are strongly fragrant, about 1 minute, then stir them into the mushroom mixture. Turn off the heat. Mix in the cream, chicken, and 1½ teaspoons salt and pour the mixture into an 8 x 8-inch baking dish.

3. To make the biscuit topping, place the almond flour, coconut flour, salt, baking soda, and baking powder in the bowl of a food processor. Pulse 2 to 3 times to combine. Add the butter and pulse for eight 1-second pulses. Pour in the coconut milk and ¼ cup cold water and pulse until the mixture comes together and forms a dough. (If the dough is too wet, add a tablespoon or two of almond flour. If it's too dry, add a teaspoon or two of water.) Use a 2-inch cookie scoop to scoop out dough balls. Place them on the top of the chicken filling, lining up the balls in a symmetrical pattern. Bake for 25 to 30 minutes, until the filling is bubbly and the biscuits are golden brown on top. Cool for 10 minutes before serving.

PALEO/DAIRY-FREE ADAPTATION: Use ½ cup cashew milk in place of the heavy cream for the filling. Use ¼ cup lard or tallow for the butter in the biscuits.

Pork Carnitas

There are those days when a slow cooker becomes your best friend. As soon as the new school year rolls around, I pull it out and let it do the work for me while I'm busy taking the kids to their activities in the afternoons. You can serve this meat by itself or topped with avocado, sour cream, and chopped tomatoes. And for a savory morning meal, you can use the leftover meat the next morning for Breakfast Crepe Tacos (page 51).

SERVES 4 TO 6

PREPARATION TIME: 10 hours

4 large yellow onions, peeled and cut into wedges

4 pounds pork shoulder

1 tablespoon Herbamare (see page 14)

1½ teaspoons paprika

1 tablespoon garlic powder

¼ teaspoon cayenne

2 teaspoons dried oregano

1 orange

Celtic sea salt and freshly ground black pepper

Place the onions in the slow cooker and top with the pork shoulder. Combine the Herbamare, paprika, garlic powder, cayenne, and oregano in a small bowl. Sprinkle all of this seasoning mix on top of the meat. Cut the orange in half, squeeze the juice over the meat, and drop the orange halves in the slow cooker (this will help give the meat more flavor). Cook on low for 10 hours, until tender. Season with salt and pepper.

Chicken Verde Enchiladas

I wouldn't have thought that savory crepes could be a good substitute for corn tortillas or hold their shape when baked in an enchilada dish, but I was wrong. They are the perfect vessel for cilantro-lime chicken and come pretty close to the real deal. The topping is a homemade roasted salsa, but don't be intimidated. You toss the vegetables with a bit of ghee, roast them, and puree. It's easy!

SERVES 4 TO 6
PREPARATION TIME: 1 hour 45 minutes

FILLING

3 bone-in, skin-on chicken breasts

½ cup chopped fresh cilantro

2 cups grated Monterey Jack cheese

Juice of ½ lime

SALSA

½ pound tomatillos, dry skins peeled off

1 onion, cut into large wedges

1 jalapeño, stem removed

4 garlic cloves

1 tablespoon ghee, melted

1 teaspoon ground cumin

1 teaspoon Celtic sea salt

Juice of 1 lime

½ cup fresh cilantro leaves

1 recipe Savory Crepes (page 277)

1. Preheat the oven to 400°F and adjust the rack to the middle position.

2. Place the chicken breasts on a baking sheet and roast for 35 to 40 minutes, or until cooked through. Set aside to cool.

3. Meanwhile, make the salsa: Place the tomatillos, onion, jalapeño, and garlic cloves on a separate large rimmed baking sheet. Toss the vegetables with the melted ghee and roast in the oven with the chicken for 20 to 25 minutes, until the vegetables are golden brown on the edges. Reduce the oven temperature to 375°F.

4. Pour the vegetables and any accumulated juices into a food processor or blender. Add the cumin, salt, lime juice, and cilantro and pulse until the mixture is a chunky salsa.

5. For the filling, remove the skin from the chicken and pull the chicken from the bones. Shred the chicken and place in a large bowl. Toss with the cilantro, 1 cup of the cheese, and the lime juice.

6. To assemble: Pour half the salsa on the bottom of an 11 x 7-inch baking dish and spread it out evenly. Place a crepe on the counter and top with ¼ cup of the chicken filling. Carefully roll the crepe around the chicken and place it in the baking dish. Repeat with the remaining chicken and crepes. Pour the remaining salsa on top of the enchiladas and sprinkle with the remaining 1 cup cheese. Bake for 25 minutes, or until golden brown and bubbly on top. Cool for 10 minutes. Serve.

PALEO/DAIRY-FREE ADAPTATION: Use lard or tallow in place of the ghee. Use 1 cup Savory Cashew "Cheese" (page 264) in place of the cheese mixture that goes inside the enchiladas. Omit the remaining cheese.

Cauliflower "Steak" with Olives, Sun-Dried Tomatoes, and Capers

Sometimes you don't want meat as the center of attention, and a thick piece of roasted cauliflower makes for a nice replacement. Some small florets are sure to fall off the cauliflower head when you cut it into thick pieces, but you can just toss those with some ghee and roast them along with the steaks.

SERVES 4

PREPARATION TIME: 35 minutes

2 heads of cauliflower

2 tablespoons ghee, melted

Celtic sea salt

½ cup extra-virgin olive oil

4 garlic cloves, minced

⅓ cup chopped kalamata olives

⅓ cup chopped oil-packed sun-dried tomatoes

¼ cup capers, drained

¼ cup chopped fresh flat-leaf parsley

1. Preheat the oven to 425°F and adjust the rack to the middle position. Line a baking sheet with unbleached parchment paper.

2. Place the cauliflower on a cutting board stem side up. Cut the cauliflower in half and then cut ½-inch-thick slices from each half.

3. Place the cauliflower slices on the prepared baking sheet. Using a pastry brush, brush melted ghee on both sides and season with salt. Roast for 10 minutes, then use tongs to turn each piece over. Continue to roast until the edges are just turning golden brown, 10 to 15 minutes.

4. Combine the olive oil, garlic, olives, tomatoes, capers, parsley, and ¼ teaspoon salt in a small bowl. Spoon the sauce over the cauliflower and serve.

PALEO/DAIRY-FREE ADAPTATION: Use lard or tallow in place of the ghee.

Sautéed Round Steak
with Onions and Mushrooms

My grandma makes a version of this in the slow cooker and it was always a favorite of mine when I was younger. Round steak can be a tough cut, but when the butcher runs it through a meat tenderizer, it becomes tender and a nice cheaper cut of meat for a weekday meal.

1. Preheat the oven to 200°F. Place a cooling rack on top of a baking sheet.

2. Place the garbanzo bean flour in a pie plate or shallow dish. Season the steaks on both sides with salt and pepper. Dredge each steak in the flour, coating both sides. Heat the ghee in a large sauté pan over medium-high heat until just shimmery. Place the steaks in the pan and cook for 2 to 3 minutes, until the bottoms are golden brown. (Don't move them or they won't get a nice golden brown crust.) Using tongs, flip the steaks and cook until the other sides are golden brown, about 4 minutes. Set the steaks on the prepared cooling rack (this keeps the crust from getting soggy) and place in the oven to keep warm.

3. Add the onions and mushrooms to the pan, lower the heat to medium-low, and sauté until the edges are just beginning to caramelize, 10 to 12 minutes. Stir in the arrowroot flour, then pour in the chicken stock and scrape the bottom of the pan with a wooden spoon to release any bits. Season with salt and pepper. Serve the onions and mushrooms over the steaks.

PALEO/DAIRY-FREE ADAPTATION: Use ½ cup almond flour in place of the garbanzo bean flour. Use coconut oil in place of the ghee.

SERVES 4
PREPARATION TIME: 30 minutes

½ cup garbanzo bean flour

4 round steaks, tenderized (ask your butcher to do this)

Celtic sea salt and freshly ground black pepper

¼ cup ghee

2 yellow onions, sliced thin

8 ounces cremini mushrooms, sliced

1 teaspoon arrowroot flour

½ cup Chicken Stock (page 252)

Roasted Garlic Cauliflower Alfredo with Chicken and Vegetables

Our dear friends the Harmons used to have our family over every Wednesday night for dinner when I was a kid. I always looked forward to it. We would eat a homemade meal, and then I'd run upstairs with my friends while the parents sat downstairs discussing everything from politics to religion. Every once in a while, fettuccine Alfredo was on the menu. I remember pouring the sauce in a thick layer over the pasta, and I just couldn't get enough of the rich, creamy flavor. At the time, we all thought fat was harmful, so my mom would give me "the look" that told me to back off.

While I still love the taste of rich cream, butter, and garlic, I like to change it up a bit and use the versatile cauliflower to create a cream base for those nights when I want something a little lighter. Now, of course we're still using organic butter in the recipe, but we all need a healthy portion of omega-3s at each meal, right?

SERVES 6

PREPARATION TIME: 1 hour

CHICKEN AND ROASTED GARLIC

2 skin-on, bone-in chicken breasts

1 garlic head, top cut off

1 teaspoon extra-virgin olive oil

VEGETABLES

4 tablespoons (½ stick) unsalted butter

1 yellow onion, chopped

8 ounces cremini mushrooms, chopped

1 cup oil-packed sun-dried tomatoes, chopped

4 cups bite-size broccoli pieces

One 10-ounce bag frozen peas, thawed

1 teaspoon Celtic sea salt

¼ teaspoon freshly ground black pepper

1. Preheat the oven to 400°F and adjust the rack to the middle position.

2. Place the chicken on a rimmed baking sheet and roast for 35 to 40 minutes, until cooked through. At the same time, set a square of foil on the counter and cover with a sheet of unbleached parchment paper. Place the garlic in the middle, drizzle the cut side with olive oil, and wrap in the parchment and foil. Roast for 30 minutes. When the chicken is cool enough to handle, remove the skin and shred the chicken. Set aside.

3. To make the vegetables, melt 2 tablespoons of the butter in a large sauté pan over medium heat and swirl to coat. Add the onion and cook until it's just turning soft, 3 to 4 minutes. Add the mushrooms and cook until they lose their moisture and begin to turn golden brown on the edges, about 10 minutes. Add the remaining 2 tablespoons butter, the sun-dried tomatoes, broccoli, and peas. Cook, stirring frequently, until the broccoli is bright green and all the ingredients are hot, about 8 minutes. Season with the salt and pepper.

4. To make the cauliflower Alfredo sauce, combine the cauliflower and chicken stock in a medium saucepan. Bring to a boil over high heat and cook until the cauliflower is tender, about 10 minutes. Transfer the cauliflower and half the chicken stock to a blender (or use a hand immersion blender) and blend until smooth. Squeeze the garlic head to release the roasted cloves and add them to the cauliflower mixture along with the butter, chopped garlic, salt, and pepper. Blend until smooth. Pour the sauce over the vegetables, then stir in the reserved chicken and the Parmesan cheese. Serve.

PALEO/DAIRY-FREE ADAPTATION: Use coconut oil in place of the butter. Use 1 cup Savory Cashew "Cheese" (page 264) in place of the butter and cheese.

CAULIFLOWER ALFREDO

6 cups chopped cauliflower

3 cups Chicken Stock (page 252)

8 tablespoons (1 stick) unsalted butter or ghee

4 garlic cloves, chopped

1 teaspoon Celtic sea salt

¼ teaspoon freshly ground black pepper

1 cup grated Parmesan cheese

Desserts

If you've been intimidated by baking, then I have good news! Grain-free baking takes all of the stress out of the baking process. You don't need to worry about ruining a recipe by mixing too long, deciphering complicated ingredients, or following a long list of steps. Most grain-free baking recipes can be made with just a bowl and spoon, or the ingredients can be whizzed together in the food processor or blender before pouring into the pan. From cookies to cakes to puddings, it's all so simple—but your guests will think you spent hours in the kitchen.

To get ready for grain-free baking you need to have a few staples on hand. The seven main ingredients are:

Almond flour	Coconut sugar
Coconut flour	Maple syrup
Arrowroot	Raw honey
Unflavored gelatin	

Once you have these basic ingredients, you're ready to bake!

I chose grain-free versions of familiar, favorite desserts for this book. While it's fun to make a new dessert, I usually find myself returning to those faithful dishes over and over, especially at the holidays or for special occasions. Thanksgiving just wouldn't feel right without a pecan pie, for instance, and we all want a bit of cake for our birthdays.

Just a note on almond flour: Different brands of almond flour can produce very different outcomes. During testing for this book we found that our favorite brand was Honeyville Farms blanched almond flour. Honeyville's flour is more finely ground than others and lends a more even texture and a finer crumb. Check the Resources section on page 283 for more information on purchasing almond flour.

Grapefruit Granita
with Minted Whipped Cream

This light, refreshing dessert can be made earlier in the day and served to guests at dinner. It's also great for a citrusy afternoon treat.

1. Combine the cream and mint in a bowl, cover, and refrigerate overnight (8 to 10 hours) to steep.

2. Combine the honey and 1 cup water in a medium saucepan over low heat. Warm the mixture until the honey is dissolved, stirring occasionally. Stir in the grapefruit juice.

3. Pour the mixture into an 8 x 8-inch baking dish and place in the freezer. Use a fork to stir the mixture every 30 minutes over the course of about 2 hours, until frozen and icy.

4. Remove the cream from the refrigerator and discard the mint. Whip the cream using a hand mixer until soft peaks form.

5. For each serving, spoon the granita into a small bowl, top with a dollop of whipped cream, and garnish with fresh mint leaves.

PALEO/DAIRY-FREE ADAPTATION: Pour a 13.5-ounce can of coconut milk into a measuring glass. Place the mint in the milk and let steep for 24 hours in the refrigerator. Spoon ½ cup of the coconut fat that has risen to the top into a bowl and whip until soft peaks form. (For further information on how to whip coconut milk, see page 270.)

SERVES 4
PREPARATION TIME: 24 hours
(most of this is steeping or freezing time)

½ **cup heavy cream**

2 fresh mint sprigs, plus more for garnish

½ **cup raw honey (I use clover)**

2½ cups fresh grapefruit juice (from 5 or 6 grapefruit)

Vanilla Pudding with Bananas and Honey-Caramel Sauce

This pudding works well with either honey or maple syrup. I chose to use raw honey in this recipe because it has a much lower glycemic index than commercial honey. If you like, you can layer the pudding with some Slice-and-Bake Cookies (page 248) and serve it in a glass trifle bowl for a pretty presentation.

SERVES 4

PREPARATION TIME: 4 hours
(most of this is chilling time)

BANANA PUDDING

1½ cups whole milk

1½ cups heavy cream

½ cup raw honey or maple syrup

¼ teaspoon Celtic sea salt

6 large egg yolks

3 tablespoons arrowroot flour

3 tablespoons unsalted butter

1 tablespoon Pure Vanilla Extract (page 274)

HONEY-CARAMEL SAUCE

4 tablespoons (½ stick) unsalted butter

½ cup raw honey

¾ cup heavy cream or coconut milk

⅛ teaspoon Celtic sea salt

½ teaspoon Pure Vanilla Extract (page 274)

2 bananas

1. To make the pudding, pour the milk, cream, ¼ cup of the honey, and the salt into a medium saucepan and heat over medium heat until just simmering.

2. Meanwhile, in a small bowl, whisk together the remaining ¼ cup honey, the egg yolks, and the arrowroot flour until creamy and smooth. When the milk mixture is simmering, slowly pour a ladleful of hot milk into the egg mixture while whisking constantly (we don't want scrambled eggs!). Again whisking constantly, slowly pour the egg mixture into the hot milk mixture in the saucepan. Continue to whisk until the mixture is thick and coats the back of a spoon, 5 to 7 minutes. Remove from the heat and stir in the butter and vanilla.

3. Pour the pudding into a bowl and place a piece of unbleached parchment paper directly on top (this keeps a skin from forming on the surface). Cool for 30 minutes at room temperature, then refrigerate for at least 3 hours.

4. To make the honey-caramel sauce, melt the butter and honey in a small saucepan over medium-low heat, stirring frequently. Whisk in the cream and bring to a strong simmer. Cook until the mixture reaches 225°F on a candy or instant-read thermometer. Remove from the heat and whisk in the salt and vanilla. Cool for 15 minutes before serving, or store in a glass jar in the refrigerator until ready to use.

continued

5. To serve: Divide the pudding among 4 dessert bowls. Top the pudding with a spoonful of caramel sauce and some sliced bananas.

PALEO/DAIRY-FREE ADAPTATION: For the pudding, use 1½ cups almond milk and 1½ cups canned coconut milk in place of the milk and heavy cream. Use 1 tablespoon palm shortening in place of the butter. For the caramel sauce, use 1 tablespoon coconut oil in place of the butter, and instead of adding it at the beginning of the recipe, add it when you whisk in the salt and vanilla.

Frozen Key Lime Pie

Every key lime pie recipe I've ever seen requires sweetened condensed milk, so for this book I developed a recipe for unprocessed sweetened condensed milk (page 275) just so I could make a key lime pie. It's important to have priorities! This pie is super simple and the flavor of fresh lime shines through.

The pie calls for half a recipe of graham crackers, so just make a batch of graham crackers, save half for this recipe, and use the other half for snacking.

1. Preheat the oven to 350°F and adjust the rack to the middle position. Butter a 9-inch pie dish.

2. Place the graham crackers in a food processor and process until finely ground. Add the melted coconut oil and process until the crumbs are uniformly wet. Press the crumbs on the bottom and up the sides of the prepared pie dish. Bake for 11 minutes. Cool.

3. In a medium bowl, whisk the egg yolks until pale yellow and creamy, about 2 minutes. Whisk in the sweetened condensed milk, zest, and lime juice until smooth. Pour into the cooled pie shell and freeze overnight. Spread whipped cream on top and serve.

NOTE: The pie filling makes for great, creamy ice pops. Just pour the filling into ice pop molds, freeze, and enjoy! If you want to serve it at a party, you can set out individual bowls of whipped cream and toasted coconut flakes to dip the ice pops in.

MAKES ONE 9-INCH PIE

PREPARATION TIME: 5 hours
(most of this is chilling time)

CRUST

Unsalted butter, for the dish

½ recipe Grain-Free Graham Crackers
(page 236)

¼ cup coconut oil, melted

LIME FILLING

6 large egg yolks

14 ounces (almost 2 cups) Sweetened
Condensed Milk (page 275)

2 tablespoons grated lime zest

½ cup plus 2 tablespoons fresh lime
juice (from 3 to 4 limes)

2 cups heavy cream or canned
coconut milk, whipped until soft
peaks form (for Whipped Coconut
Milk, see page 270)

Honey-Sweetened Cheesecake

This cheesecake can be made weeks in advance, covered tightly, and stored in the freezer. Thaw in the refrigerator for twenty-four hours before serving.

MAKES ONE 9-INCH CHEESECAKE
PREPARATION TIME: 12 hours
(almost all of this is baking or chilling time)

GRAHAM CRACKER CRUST

1 recipe Grain-Free Graham Crackers (page 236)

8 tablespoons (1 stick) unsalted butter, melted

CHEESECAKE FILLING

1 cup raw honey

Five 8-ounce packages cream cheese

2 tablespoons arrowroot flour

5 large eggs plus 2 large egg yolks

¼ cup heavy cream

1 tablespoon Pure Vanilla Extract (page 274)

BERRY TOPPING

2 pints berries (optional)

1. Preheat the oven to 350°F and adjust the rack to the middle position.

2. Place the graham crackers and butter in the bowl of a food processor. Process until the crackers are finely ground and the mixture sticks together when pressed between your fingers. Press the moist crumbs on the bottom and up the sides of a 9-inch springform pan. Bake for 12 minutes.

3. Place the honey, cream cheese, and arrowroot flour in the bowl of a standing mixer and beat on medium speed for 30 seconds, until the mixture is smooth. With the mixer on low, beat in the eggs and yolks, one at a time. Using a large spoon, stir in the cream and vanilla.

4. Pour the filling into the prepared crust and bake for 10 minutes. Lower the heat to 250°F and bake for an additional 1 hour 30 minutes. The center will jiggle a bit and the outsides will be more firm. (Don't worry, the center will set as it cools.) Cool to room temperature, then cover tightly and refrigerate overnight.

5. Before serving, push the bottom of the pan up to release the cheesecake. Place the cheesecake on a serving platter. Top with berries, if using, and serve.

PALEO/DAIRY-FREE ADAPTATION: For the crust, use 6 tablespoons coconut oil in place of the butter. For the filling ingredients, use 3 cups cashews, soaked overnight and drained, ¾ cup coconut milk (at room temperature), ¾ cup raw honey, ¾ cup coconut oil, and 1 tablespoon vanilla extract. Blend until smooth and pour into the baked crust (you do not bake this version of the filling). Refrigerate for about 4 hours, until firm. Serve with berries.

Doughnut Holes with Maple Glaze

My brother Erik has been eating a grain-free diet for some time now, and one weekend when he was in town I asked him what he missed the most. "Doughnuts," he replied.

Later that day my sister-in-law Hayle and I were cooking and the light bulb came on. We mixed, scooped, and fried up some doughnuts, crossing our fingers that it would work. It was quite a fun moment as we each bit into a hot, sweet glazed doughnut. None of us ever thought we'd be able to eat a grain-free doughnut that was just as good as the real thing.

MAKES ABOUT 20 DOUGHNUTS
PREPARATION TIME: 45 minutes

DOUGH

2 pounds (about 4 cups) lard or tallow

1 cup canned coconut milk

2 cups tapioca flour

¼ teaspoon Celtic sea salt

5 tablespoons coconut flour

3 tablespoons ghee, melted

2 large eggs

GLAZE

1 cup maple sugar

1 tablespoon arrowroot flour

2 to 3 tablespoons whole milk

½ teaspoon Pure Vanilla Extract (page 274)

1. Heat the lard or tallow in a large Dutch oven over medium-high heat until it reaches 350°F. Preheat the oven to 200°F and set a cooling rack on a baking sheet.

2. Pour the coconut milk into a medium saucepan and bring to a simmer over medium heat. Pour in the tapioca flour and stir until the flour absorbs the milk, about 2 minutes. (At this point the mixture will be a big, sticky mass of flour and milk. Don't worry!) Transfer the flour mixture to the bowl of a food processor. Add the salt, coconut flour, and ghee, turn on the machine, and process until the mixture begins to smooth out, about 20 seconds. With the motor running, add the eggs and process 1 more minute, until smooth.

3. Using a 1½-inch cookie scoop, spoon portions of dough into the hot oil. Fry the doughnuts until they are golden brown on the bottom, about 2 minutes. Using a slotted spoon, carefully turn the doughnuts over and fry until the other side is golden brown, another 1 or 2 minutes. Place the doughnuts on the prepared cooling rack and set the baking sheet in the oven to keep warm. Repeat to make the rest of the doughnuts.

4. Place the maple sugar and arrowroot flour in a coffee or spice grinder and grind until the sugar is a fine powder, about 30 seconds. Pour the sugar mixture into a bowl and stir in 2 tablespoons of the milk and the vanilla extract, mixing until the glaze is smooth. Add more milk if needed to achieve a thick, pourable glaze. Drizzle the maple glaze over the doughnuts and serve hot.

PALEO/DAIRY-FREE ADAPTATION: Use coconut oil in place of the ghee. For the glaze, use almond milk in place of the whole milk.

Carrot Cake Cupcakes with Cream Cheese Frosting

This batter also makes a nice cake. You can serve the cupcakes without the frosting for breakfast as carrot cake muffins.

MAKES 24 CUPCAKES OR MUFFINS
PREPARATION TIME: 1 hour

CARROT CUPCAKES

2 cups almond flour

½ cup coconut flour

1¼ teaspoons Grain-Free Baking Powder (page 272)

1 teaspoon baking soda

½ teaspoon Celtic sea salt

2 teaspoons ground cinnamon

1 teaspoon ground ginger

½ teaspoon ground nutmeg

1 pound carrots, grated

4 large eggs, room temperature

½ cup raw honey

1 cup coconut oil, melted

½ cup whole-milk yogurt, at room temperature

1 cup walnuts (optional)

½ cup raisins (optional)

1. Preheat the oven to 375°F and adjust the rack to the middle position. Line two 12-cup muffin pans with muffin liners.

2. Place the almond and coconut flours, baking powder, baking soda, salt, cinnamon, ginger, and nutmeg in the bowl of a standing mixer. Using the beater attachment, combine the ingredients on low for about 20 seconds. Add the grated carrots and beat on low for about 30 seconds, until incorporated.

3. Pour the eggs and honey into the bowl of a food processor or blender and process for 20 seconds. Add the melted coconut oil and yogurt and process for an additional 20 seconds, until smooth. Pour the egg mixture into the flour mixture and beat on low until combined. Spoon the batter into the muffin cups, filling each about three-quarters full. Bake for 18 to 20 minutes, or until the edges are just golden brown. Cool completely. If using as muffins, you can freeze them in an airtight container for up to 3 months. Reheat in a 300°F oven for about 10 minutes (you can put them in straight from the freezer).

4. To make the frosting, whisk the mascarpone or cream cheese, honey, and vanilla in the bowl of a standing mixer until smooth. Using a spatula, fold in the whipped cream. Frost the cooled cupcakes. These are best served the day they are made.

PALEO/DAIRY-FREE ADAPTATION: For the cupcakes, use ½ cup canned coconut or almond milk yogurt in place of the yogurt. For the frosting, use 1 cup Sweet Cashew "Cheese" (page 265) in place of the cream cheese and reduce the honey to 2 tablespoons.

NOTE: To make a cake, pour batter into a buttered 9-inch cake pan and bake at 375°F for 35 to 40 minutes, or until a cake tester inserted in the middle of the cake comes out clean.

FROSTING

¾ **pound mascarpone or cream cheese**

¼ **cup raw honey**

2 **teaspoons Pure Vanilla Extract (page 274)**

1 **cup heavy cream or canned coconut milk, whipped until soft peaks form (for Whipped Coconut Milk, see page 270)**

Chia Seed Pudding

Chia seeds are high in omega-3 fatty acids and contain alpha-linolenic acid (ALA) and linoleic acid (LA). They also contain protein, fiber, and some antioxidants. Chia seeds don't need to be ground up like flax-seeds for the body to absorb their nutrients. They absorb lots of liquid and turn very gelatinous (similar to tapioca). This pudding has a mousse-like consistency and takes only a few minutes to mix together. I prefer to eat it at room temperature because when it's chilled, the texture becomes a bit too gelatinous. If you refrigerate the pudding, make sure to leave it out for about 15 minutes to take the chill off. It's great with berries or a little whipped cream.

In a medium bowl, whisk the coconut milk, maple syrup, and extracts until smooth. Stir in the chia seeds. Divide the mixture evenly among 4 glasses. Let sit at room temperature for 2 hours. Serve with berries.

NOTE: If you'd like to make the pudding ahead of time, cover tightly and chill in the refrigerator. Set the pudding out 15 minutes before serving. It's best if eaten within 24 hours.

SERVES 4

PREPARATION TIME: 2 hours
(most of this is chilling time)

1½ cups canned coconut milk

¼ cup maple syrup or honey (or substitute a few drops of stevia)

1 tablespoon Pure Vanilla Extract (page 274)

½ teaspoon almond extract

⅓ cup chia seeds

½ cup berries

Lemon Bars

One hot summer day in Dallas when I was six years old, I asked my mom if I could make a batch of lemon bars and sell them to the neighbors. She said yes, so I happily mixed and stirred in the kitchen, baked a batch of lemon bars, cut them into squares, and walked door-to-door selling them for twenty-five cents each. I sold out within about fifteen minutes, came home, and started again. I think that day was a foreshadowing of what was to come later in life. To this day, a tangy-sweet lemon bar is one of my favorite desserts.

It's best to use organic lemons in this recipe since the zest of the lemon is baked into the filling.

SERVES 9
PREPARATION TIME: 1 hour,
plus 5 hours for chilling

CRUST

2 cups almond flour

3 tablespoons coconut flour

1 teaspoon unflavored grass-fed gelatin

¼ cup coconut sugar

1 teaspoon arrowroot flour

8 tablespoons (1 stick) cold unsalted butter, cut into tablespoons

LEMON FILLING

8 tablespoons (1 stick) unsalted butter

½ cup raw honey (I prefer a light honey, such as clover)

4 large eggs plus 3 large egg yolks

¼ cup grated lemon zest (from about 4 lemons)

½ cup fresh lemon juice (from about 4 lemons)

⅛ teaspoon Celtic sea salt

1. Preheat the oven to 350°F and adjust the rack to the middle position. Cut 2 long pieces of unbleached parchment paper, 8 inches by about 18 inches. Fit one piece of parchment into a 8 x 8-inch baking pan, pushing it into the corners and up the sides of the pan, and allowing the excess to hang over the pan edges. Lay the other piece of parchment across the first and tuck it into the corners so that all four sides are draped with parchment. (This keeps the bars from sticking and will give you the ability to lift the baked bars out of the pan for even cutting.)

2. Place the almond flour, coconut flour, gelatin, coconut sugar, and arrowroot flour in the bowl of a food processor and pulse 4 or 5 times to incorporate. Add the butter and pulse for eight 1-second pulses, or until the mixture looks like wet sand. Process again until the mixture forms a firm dough.

3. Spoon the dough into the prepared baking dish and press evenly to cover the bottom of the pan. Bake for 12 minutes, or until the crust is just turning golden brown on the edges. Let cool while you make the lemon filling.

4. Place the butter, honey, eggs and yolks, lemon zest and juice, and salt in the top of a double boiler (or place a heat-proof glass bowl over a small pot of simmering water). Whisk continuously until the mix-

ture turns thick, like a pudding, about 6 minutes. Quickly pour the filling over the crust.

5. Bake for 20 to 23 minutes, or until the filling is set on the edges. It will still jiggle a bit in the middle when shaken, but don't worry—the filling will set as it cools. Cool to room temperature, then refrigerate for at least 5 hours. Cut into bars and serve.

PALEO/DAIRY-FREE ADAPTATION: For the crust ingredients, use 6 tablespoons coconut oil in place of the butter. For the filling ingredients, use 6 tablespoons coconut oil in place of the butter.

Classic Yellow Cake with Buttercream Frosting

We all need a classic recipe we can use for layer cakes or cupcakes to help celebrate birthdays and other occasions. Layer it with buttercream frosting or change things up with lightly sweetened whipped cream, berries, or jam. The frosting requires a candy thermometer and a bit of whipping, but I promise it's worth the effort. I've made this frosting for every one of my daughters' birthday parties and the moms always stay so they can have a slice of cake with the dreamy buttercream frosting. It's that good! This batter can also be made into sixteen regular-size cupcakes. For cupcakes, reduce the baking time to 25 minutes.

SERVES 10

PREPARATION TIME: 3 hours
(most of this is baking or cooling time)

YELLOW CAKE

5 tablespoons unsalted butter, grated with a cheese grater, plus more for the pan

1 cup coconut flour, plus more for the pan

8 large eggs

½ cup raw honey (I use clover)

½ teaspoon Celtic sea salt

1 teaspoon baking soda

½ cup plain whole-milk yogurt or cultured coconut yogurt

1 tablespoon Pure Vanilla Extract (page 274)

1. Preheat the oven to 350°F and adjust the rack to the middle position. Butter a 9-inch round cake pan and dust with coconut flour (this will keep the cake from sticking).

2. Place the eggs and honey in the bowl of a standing mixer. Mix on medium-high for 5 to 7 minutes, until pale yellow and fluffy. Add the grated butter and mix for 1 minute, or until incorporated (the mixture will be lumpy). Sift the coconut flour, salt, and baking soda over the egg mixture and mix on low until combined, about 1 minute. Fold in the yogurt and vanilla.

3. Pour the batter into the buttered cake pan and bake for 30 to 35 minutes, or until the cake is just turning golden brown on top and a cake tester inserted in the middle comes out clean. Cool for 10 minutes, then run a knife around the edges and invert the cake onto a cake platter. Cool completely.

4. To make the frosting, in the bowl of a standing mixer, combine the eggs, honey, vanilla, and salt. Set the bowl over a pot of simmering water and cook, whisking constantly, until the mixture reaches 160°F, 3 to 5 minutes. Put the bowl back in the standing mixer with the whisk attachment and beat the egg mixture on medium-high until light and billowy, about 5 minutes. Reduce the speed to medium and add the

butter 1 tablespoon at a time. When all of the butter has been added, whisk the frosting for 1 minute on high until light and fluffy.

5. To assemble, using a long serrated knife, very carefully cut the cake in half lengthwise to create two layers. Set one layer on a cake stand, cut side up, and spread half the frosting evenly over the cake. Top with the second layer, cut side down, and use the remaining frosting to frost the top of the cake.

PALEO/DAIRY-FREE ADAPTATION: For the cake, use coconut oil in place of the butter. For the frosting, use palm shortening in place of the butter.

NOTE: Coconut flour absorbs a lot of moisture, so recipes using it will call for what seems like an excessive amount of eggs.

BUTTERCREAM FROSTING

4 large eggs

½ cup raw honey (I use clover)

2 teaspoons Pure Vanilla Extract (page 274)

Pinch of Celtic sea salt

1 pound (4 sticks) unsalted butter, softened, each stick cut into tablespoons

Apricot Pecan Cookies

My mom is famous for the cookie dough she sells at her shop in Dallas, The Festive Kitchen, and my all-time favorite is the apricot, oatmeal, and pecan cookie dough. With this grain-free version, I get to indulge in my favorite cookie again. The best part is that you can freeze the dough after it's been scooped into dough balls and bake the cookies straight from the freezer—just add about 3 minutes to the baking time. During the holidays I make the dough weeks in advance and pop the cookies into the oven as soon as my guests arrive, filling the house with that fresh-baked cookie smell.

1. Preheat the oven to 350°F and adjust the rack to the middle position. Line a baking sheet with unbleached parchment paper.

2. Place the almond flour, coconut flour, baking soda, gelatin, salt, and cinnamon in a large mixing bowl and stir to combine. Place the butter, honey, and almond butter in a small saucepan over medium-low heat and let the butter melt, stirring occasionally. Pour the wet mixture into the dry mixture, add the vanilla, and stir until combined. Stir in the pecans and apricots.

3. Using a 2-inch cookie scoop, scoop the dough into balls and place them on the prepared baking sheet. Using your fingers, gently press each dough ball until you have a 3-inch round. Bake for 11 to 12 minutes, or until the cookies are just turning golden brown on the edges. Cool for 15 minutes before serving. Store the cookies in an airtight container for up to 3 days.

PALEO/DAIRY-FREE ADAPTATION: Use 5 tablespoons coconut oil plus 1 tablespoon water in place of the butter.

NOTE: If you'd like to freeze the cookie dough, simply scoop all of the dough balls onto a baking sheet lined with unbleached parchment paper. Freeze the tray for 2 hours, or until the dough balls are firm. Transfer the dough balls to an airtight container and freeze for up to 3 months.

MAKES TWELVE 3-INCH COOKIES
PREPARATION TIME: 45 minutes

2 cups almond flour

2 tablespoons coconut flour

½ teaspoon baking soda

½ teaspoon unflavored grass-fed gelatin

½ teaspoon Celtic sea salt

1 teaspoon ground cinnamon

6 tablespoons unsalted butter, melted

¼ cup raw honey

2 tablespoons almond butter

1 tablespoon Pure Vanilla Extract (page 274)

¼ cup chopped pecans

¼ cup chopped apricots

Cheesecake Ice Cream

My friend Karin insisted I include this recipe in the book. She's made it for countless guests and says they all rave about it. It really is quite the treat. You can serve it alone or with berries, caramel, or crushed cookies. I like to serve it with a Homemade Waffle Cone or bowl (page 211) for an extra-special touch.

MAKES 1 QUART
PREPARATION TIME: 4 hours
(most of this is chilling or freezing time)

1½ cups whole milk

2½ cups heavy cream

¾ cup maple syrup

8 ounces cream cheese, room temperature

4 large egg yolks

2 teaspoons Pure Vanilla Extract (page 274)

1. In a large saucepan over medium heat, heat the milk, cream, and maple syrup until steaming (but don't let it burn).

2. Meanwhile, place the cream cheese, egg yolks, and vanilla in a mixing bowl and beat with an electric mixer until smooth (don't worry if it's a bit lumpy). With the mixer running, pour about ½ cup of the hot milk mixture into the cream cheese mixture, mix until incorporated, then pour all the cream cheese mixture into the remaining hot milk mixture in the saucepan and whisk until thick, 4 or 5 minutes. Pour into a large bowl and chill completely.

3. When very cold, pour the mixture into the bowl of an ice cream maker and freeze according to the manufacturer's instructions.

PALEO/DAIRY-FREE ADAPTATION: Substitute 1½ cups almond milk and 2½ cups canned coconut milk for the milk and cream. Use 1 cup Sweet Cashew "Cheese" (page 265) and 1 tablespoon lemon juice in place of the cream cheese.

Homemade Waffle Cones

This recipe requires a special appliance, but it's such a special treat I just had to include it. Eating ice cream is always fun, but if it can be scooped into a sweet, crispy container it's even better. Depending on the occasion, I'll use this batter to make waffle cones or waffle bowls. They do tend to become a bit soft after twenty-four hours, so make the cones on the same day you'll serve them. If that isn't possible you can freshen them up in a 300°F oven for 8 minutes and they'll turn nice and crispy again.

1. Preheat the waffle cone iron. In a large mixing bowl, whisk the egg whites and sugar until combined. Let sit for 1 minute, then whisk for another 10 to 15 seconds (this will help the sugar dissolve completely). Whisk in the vanilla, salt, almond flour, and melted butter.

2. Using a ladle, pour a small portion of the batter onto the hot waffle cone iron. Cook according to the manufacturer's instructions.

3. To make a cone: Roll a warm waffle around the cone maker. Set aside to cool. To make a bowl: Place a muffin tin upside down on the counter. Place a warm waffle on top of a muffin cup and gently press around the edges to create a bowl (I wear oven mitts to avoid burning my hands). Hold for about 20 seconds, release, and let cool.

PALEO/DAIRY-FREE ADAPTATION: Use 5 tablespoons coconut oil in place of the butter.

NOTE: Use the extra yolks for Cheesecake Ice Cream (page 208) or add them to your morning smoothies.

MAKES ABOUT 12 WAFFLE CONES
PREPARATION TIME: 30 minutes

8 large egg whites (see Note)

½ cup maple sugar

1 tablespoon Pure Vanilla Extract (page 274)

½ teaspoon Celtic sea salt

2½ cups almond flour

8 tablespoons (1 stick) butter, melted

Lemon Poppy Seed Cake with Honey-Coconut Glaze

Everyone needs a Bundt cake recipe in their repertoire. They're easy to prepare and always a hit at parties or holiday gatherings. When I flavor a cake, I want it to be front and center, and the combination of fresh lemon juice and zest gives this cake a bright, clean, vibrant taste. The cake can be served with or without the glaze.

1. Preheat the oven to 350°F and butter a 10-cup Bundt pan.

2. To make the cake, place the honey and eggs in the bowl of a standing mixer with the beater attachment. Beat the mixture at medium-high speed for 5 minutes, until pale and fluffy. Turn the speed to medium and slowly pour in the cooled butter, vanilla, and lemon juice.

3. Sift the almond flour, coconut flour, baking soda, and baking powder into a large bowl. Stir in the salt, lemon zest, and poppy seeds. Gently fold the dry mixture into the wet mixture until incorporated. Pour into the Bundt pan and bake for 30 to 35 minutes, or until a cake tester inserted in the middle of the cake comes out clean. Cool for 10 minutes, then invert onto a cooling rack or cake platter.

4. To make the glaze, place the coconut butter, honey, lemon zest and juice, vanilla bean seeds, and 2 tablespoons water in a small saucepan over low heat. Cook until the mixture becomes a warm, smooth glaze. Pour over the cake (you can glaze the cake 4 to 5 hours ahead of time). Serve.

PALEO/DAIRY-FREE ADAPTATION: Use 6 tablespoons coconut oil plus 1 tablespoon water in place of the butter.

SERVES 12

PREPARATION TIME: 1 hour
(most of this is baking time)

LEMON POPPY SEED CAKE

Unsalted butter for the pan

⅔ cup raw honey

6 large eggs

8 tablespoons (1 stick) unsalted butter, melted and cooled

1 tablespoon Pure Vanilla Extract (page 274)

½ cup fresh lemon juice (from about 4 lemons)

4½ cups almond flour

2 tablespoons coconut flour

2 teaspoons baking soda

1 teaspoon Grain-Free Baking Powder (page 272)

½ teaspoon Celtic sea salt

½ cup grated lemon zest (from about 8 to 10 lemons)

2 tablespoons poppy seeds

HONEY-COCONUT GLAZE

½ cup Coconut Butter (page 273)

2 tablespoons raw honey

Grated zest of 1 lemon

¼ cup lemon juice (from 2 to 3 lemons)

Seeds scraped from 1 vanilla bean (or 1 teaspoon Pure Vanilla Extract, page 274)

Blackberry Apple Crisp

Apples and blackberries are my favorite combination in any cobbler or crisp. I usually use frozen blackberries, but if you can get your hands on some fresh organic berries, by all means use those. I like to serve this with a spoonful of Cheesecake Ice Cream (page 208) or sweetened whipped cream.

1. Preheat the oven to 350°F and adjust the rack to the middle position. Butter a 2-quart baking dish.

2. In a large bowl, combine the apples, blackberries, lemon and orange zests, lemon and orange juices, arrowroot flour, coconut sugar, and cinnamon. Pour the fruit into the prepared baking dish.

3. To make the topping, pulse the almond flour, coconut flour, gelatin, coconut sugar, honey, and salt in a food processor for four 1-second pulses. Add the butter and pulse for ten 1-second pulses, until the butter is incorporated. Add the coconut flakes and pulse again 3 or 4 times to thoroughly combine. Using your hands, scatter the crumb topping evenly over the fruit.

4. Bake for 35 to 40 minutes, until the top is golden brown and the fruit is bubbly. Serve warm with a dollop of whipped cream on top, if desired.

PALEO/DAIRY-FREE ADAPTATION: Use 6 tablespoons frozen palm shortening (see page 12) cut into tablespoons for the butter.

SERVES 8
PREPARATION TIME: 1 hour

FILLING

Unsalted butter for the baking dish

3 apples, preferably Gala, peeled, cored, and cut into large bite-size pieces

2 cups blackberries, fresh or frozen

Grated zest of 1 lemon

Grated zest of 1 orange

2 tablespoons lemon juice

2 tablespoons orange juice

1 tablespoon arrowroot flour

¼ cup coconut sugar

½ teaspoon ground cinnamon

TOPPING

1 cup almond flour

2 tablespoons coconut flour

½ teaspoon unflavored grass-fed gelatin

½ cup coconut sugar

1 tablespoon raw honey

¼ teaspoon Celtic sea salt

8 tablespoons (1 stick) cold unsalted butter, cut into tablespoons

½ cup unsweetened coconut flakes

½ cup heavy cream or canned coconut milk, whipped until soft peaks form (for Whipped Coconut Milk, see page 270) (optional)

Madeleines

My favorite kind of cookie is subtly sweet, without any fancy bits, and madeleines fit the bill. They're a nice addition to tea, a ladies' brunch, or the holiday breakfast table. A madeleine pan is needed for this recipe, but if you don't own one a mini muffin or doughnut pan will do nicely.

MAKES 12 COOKIES

PREPARATION TIME: 45 minutes

Unsalted butter for the pan

4 large eggs

$2/3$ cup maple sugar

8 tablespoons (1 stick) unsalted butter, melted and cooled

¼ cup plus 1 tablespoon coconut flour

2 tablespoons arrowroot flour

1 teaspoon Pure Vanilla Extract (page 274)

1. Preheat the oven to 375°F and adjust the rack to the middle position. Thoroughly butter a madeleine pan.

2. Place the eggs and maple sugar in the bowl of a standing mixer with a whisk attachment. Whisk on medium-high for 8 minutes, then slowly whisk in the cooled butter. Sift the coconut flour and arrowroot flour over the egg mixture and gently fold in until incorporated. Stir in the vanilla. Let the batter sit for 20 minutes at room temperature.

3. Spoon the batter into the buttered pan. Bake for 11 minutes, or until just turning golden brown on the edges. As soon as the cookies come out of the oven, invert the pan onto a cooling rack to release the madeleines. Serve at room temperature.

PALEO/DAIRY-FREE ADAPTATION: Use 6 tablespoons coconut oil and 1 tablespoon of water in place of the butter.

Pecan Pie

Pecan pie is the epitome of Thanksgiving for me. After a savory meal, I get a cup of coffee and a slice of pecan pie, then sit back and enjoy the conversation around the table. The filling in my pecan pie isn't cloyingly sweet, just nice and subtle. The pecans are crunchy on top and the crust is tender and buttery.

Nut flours can brown very quickly in the oven, so place a pie shield (foil will also do) around the edge of the crust to keep it from burning. You can bake the pie in a 9-inch pie pan or make things a bit fancier with a tart pan. The filling can be made weeks in advance and stored in the freezer. Thaw it completely before pouring it into the pie crust and topping with pecan halves.

MAKES ONE 9-INCH PIE
PREPARATION TIME: 1 hour

1 cup plus 1 tablespoon pure maple syrup

½ cup maple sugar

2 tablespoons unsalted butter, room temperature

3 large eggs, lightly beaten

1 teaspoon Pure Vanilla Extract (page 274)

¼ teaspoon Celtic sea salt

1 Grain-Free Piecrust (page 268)

1 to 1¼ cups whole pecan halves

1. Preheat the oven to 400°F and adjust the rack to the lower-middle position.

2. Heat the maple syrup over medium heat in a medium saucepan. Simmer until the syrup reaches 225°F on a candy thermometer, 10 to 15 minutes. While the syrup is simmering, place the maple sugar and butter in a medium bowl and stir to combine. As soon as the syrup reaches 225°F, immediately pour it over the sugar and butter. Let the mixture sit for 1 minute, then whisk together. Whisk in the eggs, vanilla, and salt (the mixture might look a little grainy at this point).

3. Place the pie plate with the prepared crust on a large baking sheet. Pour the mixture into the crust and top with the pecans in a pretty circular pattern. Cover just the crust with a pie shield or foil to keep it from burning. Bake for 15 minutes, lower the heat to 350°F, and bake for 15 minutes more, until the edges of the filling are set. The filling will be slightly less set in the center than at the edges. It also might puff up in the middle, but will set as it cools. Serve slightly warm or at room temperature. And if you're feeling fancy, a dollop of whipped cream makes for a lovely topping.

PALEO/DAIRY-FREE ADAPTATION: Use coconut oil in place of the butter.

Baked Pears and Cream

I remember my mom making this dessert for dinner guests often, and now I realize why—it's a subtly sweet, easy-to-assemble dessert that can be served any time of year. You can substitute peaches, nectarines, apricots, or apples for the pears, depending on what looks good or is in season.

1. Preheat the oven to 400°F and adjust the rack to the middle position.

2. Pour half the butter and half the maple syrup in a shallow baking dish. Place the pears in the dish cut side down and pour the remaining butter and syrup over them. Bake for 10 minutes. Pour the cream over the pears and bake for 10 minutes more. Serve the pears warm, drizzled with the sweet cream from the dish.

PALEO/DAIRY-FREE ADAPTATION: Use coconut oil in place of the butter. Use ¼ cup canned coconut milk in place of the cream.

NOTE: To change the flavors a bit in this recipe, you can add cinnamon, ginger, or pumpkin pie spice to the butter and syrup, or add a splash of amaretto or brandy just before serving. Plumped raisins tossed on top would also make a nice addition.

SERVES 4

PREPARATION TIME: 30 minutes

2 tablespoons unsalted butter, melted

2 tablespoons maple syrup or honey

2 Bosc or Bartlett pears, halved lengthwise

¼ cup heavy cream

Ice Cream and Apricot Slice

My mom used to make this each year on the Fourth of July. We'd pack up the car with homemade goodies and head to a friend's house to grill hamburgers, swim, and watch the fireworks. The highlight of my day was always the ice cream and apricot slice. The secret is all in the almond extract. It's blended with the apricot preserves to make for a dynamite combination with homemade ice cream and a sweet pecan crust.

SERVES 9

PREPARATION TIME: 5 hours
(most of this is freezing time)

3 cups finely chopped pecans

⅓ cup coconut sugar

8 tablespoons (1 stick) unsalted butter, melted

2 cups apricot preserves

1 teaspoon almond extract

1 recipe Cheesecake Ice Cream (page 208) or 1 quart good homemade vanilla ice cream, softened

1. Preheat the oven to 400°F and adjust the rack to the middle position.

2. Mix the pecans, sugar, and butter in a bowl until combined thoroughly. Press the mixture into the bottom of an 11 x 7-inch baking dish. Bake for 12 minutes, until golden brown. Set aside to cool completely.

3. Whisk the preserves and extract in a small bowl and spread the mixture evenly over the crust. Place in the freezer for 30 minutes until the preserves are stiff (the preserves won't freeze completely).

4. Spread the ice cream evenly over the apricot mixture. Return to the freezer and freeze until hard, at least 3 hours. Cut into slices and serve frozen.

PALEO/DAIRY-FREE ADAPTATION: Use coconut oil in place of the butter.

Kids' Favorites

As you might imagine, we talk about food and cooking a lot at my house. But it's not just because it's my hobby, or even my personal passion. We talk about it because understanding nutrition is important—it's the foundation for building a healthy life. Teaching my kids where food comes from and how to prepare it in the healthiest ways is a gift that will benefit them their entire lives.

I have two daughters, currently ages eleven and twelve, and I want to give them the skills they need to one day cook on their own, and hopefully in the future for their own families. We've gone over kitchen basics like proper knife skills and how to cook at the stove. I've shown them how to shop at the store, compare prices, and pick the healthiest foods we can afford. As we work together in the kitchen, I've educated them about factory farms and why we've decided to purchase organic, pastured meats for our family. I read Michael Pollan's *The Omnivore's Dilemma: The Secrets Behind What You Eat* (the young readers edition) out loud to the kids when they were about seven and eight years old, which led to family discussions about GMOs, fast foods, and food dyes. Working together in the kitchen is the perfect setting for these conversations.

When it comes down to it, though, my girls are just normal kids. They might know a little more than their friends about pesticides and preservatives, but they still love to eat things like chicken nuggets and macaroni and cheese. That's why I asked them for their favorite foods when creating this chapter on kid-friendly, grain-free foods.

"Tortilla" soup has been a favorite since they were young—they especially love taking it to school in an insulated container for lunch. They also love taking their homemade fruit snacks to show off all the fun colors and shapes. For birthday parties they often request chicken nuggets—I've fed these nuggets to dozens of young kids, and they're always a hit. The other kids never suspect that they're grain free. And of course, what child doesn't want slice-and-bake cookies to decorate around the holidays?

PACKING LUNCHES

Packing healthy lunches for school isn't complicated, but it helps to have some key lunch-packing gear on hand. Here are a few items that I've found useful for packing food to go. (See the Resources section on page 283 for detailed shopping information.)

Insulated thermoses—We reheat soups or leftovers and put them in these containers for a nutritious hot lunch. These thermoses are great for cold foods like smoothies and puddings as well.

Stainless-steel or glass water bottles—These bottles are reusable and last for many years. I prefer stainless steel or glass because you don't have to worry about any plastic chemicals leaching into the liquid.

Lunchskins—These little bags replace all those plastic baggies in the kitchen. They're made of food-safe materials and have a Velcro seal so they're perfect for packing dry foods to take to school, the pool, or the park. They're also dishwasher safe!

Stainless steel lunch containers—These come in all shapes and sizes and are basically indestructible. They're dishwasher safe, leak proof, and worry free because there are no BPAs or other chemicals leaching into the food.

Granola

Homemade granola makes a great stand-in for boxed cereal and is much more nutritious. I make it on the weekends and keep it in a large glass jar so the kids can pour some into a bowl and top it with milk for a quick breakfast or snack. You can reduce the amount of honey by ⅓ cup if desired, or substitute maple or coconut sugar.

1. Preheat the oven to 170°F and adjust the rack to the middle position. Line a baking sheet with unbleached parchment paper.

2. Place the almonds, cashews, coconut, and seeds in a large mixing bowl. In a small saucepan over medium heat, bring the oil, honey, and salt to a simmer. Stir in the vanilla and pour over the nut mixture. Fold until incorporated.

3. Pour the mixture onto the prepared baking sheet and spread it out evenly. Bake for 7 to 8 hours, or until just turning golden brown. Cool completely. Keep in an airtight container for 2 to 3 weeks.

MAKES ABOUT 5 CUPS

PREPARATION TIME: 45 minutes

1½ cups chopped soaked and dehydrated almonds (page 276)

1½ cups chopped soaked and dehydrated cashews (page 276)

1 cup shredded unsweetened coconut

1½ cups seeds (I use soaked and dehydrated pumpkin and sunflower seeds, page 276)

3 tablespoons coconut oil or unsalted butter, melted

⅔ cup light raw honey or a few drops of stevia

¼ teaspoon Celtic sea salt

1 tablespoon Pure Vanilla Extract (page 274)

Nut- or Seed-Butter Shake

I try to incorporate raw egg yolks into our meals a few times a week. Organic, pastured egg yolks are a rich source of carotenoids, omega-3 fatty acids, and fat-soluble antioxidant nutrients. When consuming raw egg yolks, I prefer to use only pastured or good-quality organic eggs for optimal nutritional value. You can't taste the egg yolk in the shake, and it gives it a creamy consistency. If you don't want to use raw yolks, however, simply omit them. This is my daughters' favorite morning shake, and it also makes for a dynamite after-school snack.

Place all the ingredients in a blender with 2 cups cold water and blend until smooth.

NOTE: You can change things up by using a combination of yogurt and milk in place of the coconut milk and adding different extracts, such as vanilla or almond. Throwing in a cup or so of ice will turn this shake into a cold, creamy slushy.

SERVES 4
PREPARATION TIME: 5 minutes

2 cups cold canned coconut milk

½ cup almond, peanut, or seed butter

1 tablespoon raw honey or maple syrup

4 large egg yolks

2 tablespoons carob powder (optional)

Chicken Nuggets

This is my kids' favorite recipe, hands down. They request it for every birthday and special occasion. You can use this same coating for chicken fried steak or for Southern fried chicken (using bone-in, skin-on chicken).

SERVES 4 OR 5
PREPARATION TIME: 45 minutes

2 pounds (about 4 cups) lard or tallow

2 cups almond flour

¼ cup coconut flour

1 tablespoon Herbamare (page 14)

1 teaspoon paprika

½ cup sprouted garbanzo bean flour

1½ teaspoons unflavored grass-fed gelatin

5 large eggs

2 pounds boneless, skinless chicken breasts, cut into bite-size pieces (about 1½ inches thick)

1. Place the lard in a large pot or Dutch oven and heat over medium-high heat to 350°F on a candy thermometer (this will take about 10 minutes).

2. Place a cooling rack on top of a baking sheet. Preheat the oven to 275°F and adjust the rack to the middle position.

3. While the lard is heating, place the almond flour, coconut flour, Herbamare, paprika, garbanzo bean flour, and gelatin in a large baking dish and toss gently to combine. Crack the eggs into a pie plate and whisk in 2 tablespoons water. Dip a few pieces of chicken first into the flour mixture, then the egg, then the flour again. Set the coated chicken on a large plate while you coat the remaining chicken.

4. When the lard is at 350°F, carefully place 8 to 10 chicken pieces in the hot oil. Fry for about 2 minutes, or until they're golden brown on the bottom. Use tongs to flip the chicken pieces. Cook until the other side is brown, about 2 minutes. As you finish the chicken pieces, place them on the prepared baking sheet. Place the sheet in the oven to keep the chicken warm while you cook the remaining chicken. Serve hot with Ranch Dressing (page 256) or Quick Homemade Ketchup (page 279).

PALEO/DAIRY-FREE ADAPTATION: Use ½ cup arrowroot flour for the garbanzo bean flour.

Grilled Cheese

How fun is a grain-free grilled cheese? Very! My kids were thrilled the first time I served these with some tomato soup for dinner. Cheddar cheese is melted between two waffles for a fun take on a classic.

MAKES 6 SANDWICHES

PREPARATION TIME: 45 minutes

½ cup raw cashews, soaked overnight and drained

1½ cups almond flour

2 tablespoons coconut flour

¾ teaspoon unflavored grass-fed gelatin

½ teaspoon Celtic sea salt

1½ teaspoons baking soda

4 large eggs

4 tablespoons (½ stick) unsalted butter, melted

1 tablespoon raw honey (I use clover)

2 teaspoons raw apple cider vinegar

2 tablespoons unsalted butter

12 ounces Cheddar cheese, shredded

1. Place the cashews and ¼ cup water in the bowl of a food processor. Process until smooth, scraping down the sides a few times to ensure that all the cashews are pureed. Add the almond flour, coconut flour, gelatin, salt, baking soda, eggs, butter, honey, and cider vinegar and process until smooth. Cook in a waffle maker according to the manufacturer's instructions. Set the cooked waffles aside to cool as you make the rest.

2. Preheat a large skillet over medium heat for 2 minutes. Butter one side of two waffles. Place the buttered side of one waffle on the hot skillet. Top with a small handful of shredded cheese. Place the second waffle butter side up on top of the cheese. Cook until the bottom of the sandwich is golden brown, about 2 minutes. Using a spatula, flip the sandwich over and press down to flatten a bit. Cook the second side until golden brown, an additional 2 minutes. Repeat to make 5 more sandwiches. Serve.

PALEO/DAIRY-FREE ADAPTATION: For the waffles, use coconut oil in place of the butter. Use ¾ cup Savory Cashew "Cheese" (page 264) in place of the Cheddar.

NOTE: You can play with the fillings in this recipe and use nut butter, bananas, or bacon as a fun food to sandwich between the waffles.

Tomato Soup

I don't know a kid who doesn't enjoy tomato soup and grilled cheese on a cold day. This soup is easy to prepare and will keep in the fridge for a few days, ready to reheat and pour into an insulated thermos for lunch the next day.

Melt the butter in a large pot or Dutch oven over medium heat. Stir in the onion, carrots, and celery, cover the pot, and turn the heat to the lowest setting. Cook the vegetables for 30 minutes, uncover, stir in the tomato paste, and cook for 5 minutes, stirring occasionally. Add the chicken stock, crushed tomatoes, and salt and stir to combine. Increase the heat to medium and bring the soup to a low simmer for 6 to 8 minutes, or until the soup is piping hot. Stir in the cream, adjust the salt to taste, and serve.

PALEO/DAIRY-FREE ADAPTATION: Use 2 tablespoons coconut oil in place of the butter. Use canned coconut milk in place of the heavy cream.

SERVES 6

PREPARATION TIME: 40 minutes

4 tablespoons (½ stick) unsalted butter

1 yellow onion, chopped

2 carrots, chopped

2 celery stalks, chopped

¼ cup tomato paste

6 cups Chicken Stock (page 252)

One 24-ounce jar crushed tomatoes

1½ teaspoons Celtic sea salt, plus more to taste

1 cup heavy cream

Grain-Free Graham Crackers

Graham crackers are a nostalgic favorite and a great foundation for homemade s'mores, a crust for your favorite pie, or just snacking.

MAKES ABOUT TWENTY 3-INCH SQUARE CRACKERS
PREPARATION TIME: 30 minutes

2 cups almond flour

¼ cup coconut flour, plus more for dusting

¾ teaspoon unflavored grass-fed gelatin

2 tablespoons raw honey (I use clover)

¾ teaspoon Grain-Free Baking Powder (page 272)

½ teaspoon baking soda

½ teaspoon Celtic sea salt

⅛ teaspoon ground cinnamon

6 tablespoons cold unsalted butter, cut into ¼-inch cubes

¼ cup molasses

3 tablespoons heavy cream or coconut milk

½ teaspoon Pure Vanilla Extract (page 274)

1. Preheat the oven to 350°F and adjust the rack to the middle position.

2. Place the flours, gelatin, honey, baking powder, baking soda, salt, and cinnamon in the bowl of a food processor and pulse 4 times to combine. Add the butter and pulse 7 times, until the mixture resembles cornmeal. Add the molasses, cream, and vanilla and process until the dough forms a ball. The dough will be very tacky. Turn the dough out onto a piece of unbleached parchment paper large enough to cover a large baking sheet.

3. Dust the top of the dough with a little coconut flour. Use a rolling pin to roll the dough out to a rectangle about 14 x 11 inches and ⅛ inch thick. Using a knife or rolling pizza cutter, cut the rectangle into about twenty 3-inch square pieces. There will be small pieces of excess on the sides (I bake them along with the crackers and eat them as a snack later). Poke holes in the top of the dough with a fork. Lift the parchment and place it on a baking sheet.

4. Bake the graham crackers for 18 to 20 minutes, or until the edges just start to darken. Let the crackers cool completely. Break them into individual crackers and store them in an airtight container. The crackers will keep for 1 week.

PALEO/DAIRY-FREE ADAPTATION: Use ¼ cup coconut oil in place of the butter. Reduce the baking time to 15 minutes.

Fruit Snacks

Most fruit snacks are loaded with sugars, food dyes, and preservatives. A simple mixture of juice and gelatin from grass-fed, pastured cows is a more nutritious alternative and very simple to make at home. Grass-fed gelatin contains 6 to 12 grams of protein per tablespoon, aids in digestion, and can contribute to the building of strong cartilage and bones. Gelatin has also been shown to benefit the digestive tract, immune system, heart, liver, muscles, and skin. And ladies, it can help smooth out those wrinkles from the inside out. No need to waste money on those expensive collagen-inducing creams—just eat some grass-fed gelatin instead!

MAKES 24 TWO-INCH FRUIT SNACKS

PREPARATION TIME: 1½ hours (most of this is chilling time)

2 cups fruit juice (cherry, orange, or juice of your choice—see Note)

⅓ cup plus 1 tablespoon unflavored gelatin

Pour the fruit juice into a medium saucepan and sprinkle the gelatin on top. Let sit for 5 minutes (the gelatin will quickly soak up the juice—it's fun for the kids to watch!). Turn the burner on low and cook, stirring frequently, until all the gelatin is dissolved, about 5 minutes. Pour the gelatin into molds (I prefer a silicone mold because it ensures the fruit snacks will pop out very easily when they're firm). Refrigerate the molds for 1 hour, or until the fruit snacks have gelled. Pop the fruit snacks out of the molds and store them in an airtight container in the refrigerator.

NOTE: If you use a tart juice such as unsweetened cherry or pomegranate, add ⅓ cup raw honey to the pan along with the juice.

Banana Maple Ice Pops

My kids love to make ice pops at home. I like to keep coconut milk, yogurt, juices, berries, and natural sweeteners on hand so they can experiment in the kitchen and come up with their own flavors.

Place all the ingredients in a blender and blend until smooth. Pour into ice pop molds and freeze according to the manufacturer's instructions.

NOTE: I recently purchased the Zoku ice pop maker and I have to say, it's quite impressive. The kids keep the Zoku maker in the freezer so whenever they feel like an ice pop, they just mix up the ingredients and pour them into the ice pop maker—then 7 minutes later they're enjoying frozen treats they made themselves!

MAKES ABOUT 9 ICE POPS

PREPARATION TIME: 3 hours
(almost all of this is freezing time)

One 13.5-ounce can coconut milk

2 bananas

2 teaspoons Pure Vanilla Extract
(page 274)

2 tablespoons maple syrup
(or a few drops of stevia)

Perfect Grain-Free Pizza Crust

This pizza crust may not contain any grain, but it's really delicious—and so easy! To serve this to a large crowd, bake the crusts early in the day, then let your guests add their own toppings before putting them back in the oven. And guess what? This dough is very similar to the doughnut recipe (page 196), with the addition of cheese. Once you master this, you can master that! This recipe was adapted from the fantastic food blog Gluten-Free on a Shoestring.

SERVES 4 (MAKES FOUR 8-INCH INDIVIDUAL PIZZAS)
PREPARATION TIME: 30 minutes

CRUST

1 cup water

2 cups tapioca flour

½ cup coconut flour

½ teaspoon Celtic sea salt

3 tablespoons extra-virgin olive oil

2 large eggs

1¼ cups shredded mozzarella cheese

TOPPINGS

¾ cup marinara sauce

2 cups shredded mozzarella cheese

Cooked sausage, chopped bell peppers, or other toppings as desired

1. Preheat the oven to 425°F and adjust the rack to the middle position. Line 2 large baking sheets with unbleached parchment paper.

2. Pour the water into a medium saucepan and bring to a simmer over medium heat. Add the tapioca flour and stir until the flour absorbs the water, about 2 minutes. (At this point the mixture will be a big, sticky mass of flour and water. Don't worry!) Transfer the flour mixture to the bowl of a food processor. Add the coconut flour, salt, and olive oil to the flour mixture. Process until the mixture begins to smooth out, about 20 seconds. With the machine running, add the eggs and cheese and process 1 minute more, until smooth.

3. Spoon the mixture onto the lined baking sheets, placing 2 mounds on each sheet. Using an offset spatula, spread each mound into an 8-inch round (about ¼ inch thick). Bake for 12 to 15 minutes, or until just golden brown on the edges.

4. Spread 2 heaping tablespoons of marinara on each crust. Top with mozzarella and any additional toppings you want. Bake for 10 minutes, or until the cheese is bubbly and just turning golden brown.

PALEO/DAIRY-FREE ADAPTATION: Omit the mozzarella cheese. For the toppings, omit the mozzarella.

"Tortilla" Soup

When I was first married my mom bought me a subscription to *Cook's Illustrated*, and I would pore over it every month, soaking up every little piece of advice they gave. I think it's one of the best food magazines out there, and I've bought subscriptions for dozens of friends. A version of this soup appeared in an issue years ago, and I adapted it for my kids to suit their growing palates. My girls asked for this soup for their birthday meal each year from age three to seven, and it's still their all-time favorite soup.

I like to serve this soup with lots of toppings, but you can pick which ones you like best. This soup also freezes very well and makes a fantastic lunch to take to school or work.

1. Place the garlic cloves in a large pot or Dutch oven over medium-high heat. Cook, stirring frequently, until the garlic begins to darken, 2 to 2½ minutes. Carefully add the chicken stock (the pot will sizzle), cilantro, and chicken. Increase the heat to high and bring the stock to a boil, then reduce to a simmer. Skim off any foam that rises to the top with a large spoon. Simmer for about 30 minutes, or until the chicken is cooked through.

2. Remove the chicken and set it aside on a plate to cool. With a slotted spoon, strain out the garlic and cilantro and discard. Remove and discard the chicken skin and bones. Shred the chicken with a fork and return it to the soup. Add salt and pepper to taste.

3. Serve the soup with the cilantro, avocado, tomatoes, sour cream, cheese, and a squeeze of lime.

PALEO/DAIRY-FREE ADAPTATION: Omit the sour cream and Cheddar cheese.

SERVES 6

PREPARATION TIME: 45 minutes

SOUP

5 garlic cloves, crushed with the skins on

2 quarts Chicken Stock (page 252)

1 handful of cilantro, with stems (about 10 sprigs)

2 pounds bone-in, skin-on chicken breasts

Celtic sea salt and freshly ground black pepper

TOPPINGS

½ cup cilantro, chopped

1 avocado, cubed

2 tomatoes, cut into bite-size chunks

½ cup sour cream

½ cup shredded Cheddar cheese

1 lime, quartered

Kids' Squash and Cheese

This recipe comes from my sweet friend Molly. Molly and her husband, John, run Apricot Lane Farms in Southern California. The farm is one of my kids' favorite places to visit—feeding the chickens, saying hi to the goats, picking ripe fruit off the trees, running wild through the pasture. It really is a magical place. Molly's Squash and Cheese is one of my kids' most requested dishes.

SERVES 6

PREPARATION TIME: 45 minutes

3 tablespoons unsalted butter, plus more for the dish

½ cup heavy cream

1 teaspoon Celtic sea salt

½ teaspoon freshly ground black pepper

Dash of cayenne

Dash of ground nutmeg

1½ cups shredded white Cheddar cheese

3 cups cooked spaghetti squash (see Note)

2 Roma (plum) tomatoes, cut into ⅛-inch slices

½ cup finely grated Parmesan cheese

2 teaspoons extra-virgin olive oil

1. Preheat the oven to 350°F and adjust the rack to the middle position. Butter an 8 x 11-inch baking dish.

2. Place the butter, cream, salt, pepper, cayenne, and nutmeg in a medium saucepan over medium heat. Bring to a simmer, stirring occasionally (be careful not to scald the cream). Whisk in the Cheddar cheese, stirring constantly until melted. Remove from the heat. Stir in the spaghetti squash, mixing until all the squash is coated with cheese sauce.

3. Pour the mixture into the prepared baking dish and spread it out evenly. Arrange the sliced tomatoes on the squash and sprinkle with Parmesan cheese. Drizzle the olive oil over the casserole and bake for 50 minutes, or until the tomatoes are roasted and edges are just turning golden brown. Cool for 10 minutes and serve.

PALEO/DAIRY-FREE ADAPTATION: Use 1 cup Savory Cashew "Cheese" (page 264) in place of the cream, salt, pepper, cayenne, nutmeg, Cheddar, and Parmesan. Instead of the directions above, melt 2 tablespoons coconut oil in a medium saucepan over medium heat. Stir in the cashew cheese and stir until incorporated. Stir in the spaghetti squash. Pour the mixture into a buttered 8 x 11-inch baking dish. Arrange the sliced tomatoes over the squash. Drizzle the olive oil over the casserole. Bake for 50 minutes, or until the tomatoes are roasted and the edges are just turning golden brown. Cool for 10 minutes and serve.

NOTE: To bake spaghetti squash, preheat the oven to 400°F. Cut the squash in half, pole-to-pole. Scoop out the seeds with a large spoon and discard. Place the squash halves cut side down in a large baking dish. Prick the skin with a fork ten times on each side. Bake for 1 hour. Use a fork to pull the flesh of the squash into "spaghetti," then measure it to use in the recipe. You can also serve it plain with a little butter, salt, and pepper or with marinara sauce.

Cut-Out or Slice-and-Bake Cookies

Eating a grain-free diet doesn't mean you have to miss out on fun holiday traditions. This dough is easy enough for the kids to make themselves and can be used for either cut-out cookies or rolled, chilled, sliced, and baked cookies. You can add chopped nuts or dried fruit to the dough for variations; a simple butter-cream frosting or some dye-free sprinkles make for a festive topping.

MAKES ABOUT 2 DOZEN COOKIES

PREPARATION TIME: About 1½ hours
(most of this is chilling or baking time)

2 cups almond flour

2 tablespoons coconut flour

½ cup organic maple sugar, whole cane sugar, or Sucanat

½ teaspoon unflavored grass-fed gelatin

1 teaspoon arrowroot flour, plus more for dusting

¾ teaspoon Celtic sea salt

8 tablespoons (1 stick) cold unsalted butter, cut into tablespoons

1. Place the almond flour, coconut flour, sugar, gelatin, arrowroot flour, and salt in the bowl of a food processor. Pulse 2 or 3 times to combine. Add the butter and process until the dough forms a ball.

For cut-out cookies:

2. Form the dough into a flat 9-inch disk. Wrap it tightly (I like to use a layer of unbleached parchment paper and then plastic wrap) and refrigerate it for at least 1 hour.

3. Preheat the oven to 350°F and adjust the rack to the middle position. Line a baking sheet with unbleached parchment paper.

4. Dust a large surface with a bit of arrowroot flour and roll the dough ¼ inch thick. Cut the dough with cookie cutters and transfer the cookies to the prepared baking sheet. Bake for 9 or 10 minutes, or until the cookies are just turning golden brown on the edges. Cool completely before serving.

For slice-and-bake cookies:

2. Form the dough into a 12-inch log and wrap it tightly (I like to use a layer of unbleached parchment paper and then plastic wrap). Refrigerate for at least 1 hour.

3. Preheat the oven to 350°F and adjust the rack to the middle position. Line a baking sheet with unbleached parchment paper.

4. Cut the dough into ¼-inch-thick slices and place on the prepared baking sheet. Bake for 9 or 10 minutes, until the cookies are just golden brown on the edges. Cool completely before serving.

PALEO/DAIRY-FREE ADAPTATION: Use 5 tablespoons frozen palm shortening (see page 12) cut into tablespoons in place of the butter. Add 1 egg to the dough mixture.

NOTE: These cookies can also be used to make linzer cookies. All you need is a linzer cookie cutter and some jam!

Basics

Many of these quality grain-free, unprocessed basics can be bought at a store, but often when they're made the proper way (without processed ingredients or excessive heat, which can destroy nutrients), the prices for these basic foods can be pretty high. So instead of paying top dollar for these simple foods, I've compiled a collection of my favorite, must-have recipes for a grain-free kitchen.

Homemade chicken stock, sauerkraut, ghee—these might sound like daunting foods to make at home, but I can assure you that they're quite simple. A friend told me she's seen ghee on my blog for months, but has been too intimidated to make it. I think many of us feel this way. When foods are unfamiliar, we tend to shy away, but I hope to take some of the fear out of these foods for you.

In our house, I make a pot of chicken stock each week to have on hand for cooking. I usu-ally put the stock on the stove before we go to bed and let it simmer and bubble away while we sleep. Commercial baking powder often contains cornstarch, so I make a batch of homemade grain-free baking powder every couple of months and store it in a glass con-tainer in the pantry.

I've also included two fermented recipes in this chapter because I believe that fermented foods are a great, highly nutritional addition to the diet. Fermented foods contain millions of good bacteria (also known as probiotics), aid in digestion, and keep our gut and immune system healthy. Fermenting is usually as sim-ple as chopping up vegetables, putting them in a jar, adding Celtic sea salt, and letting them sit for a few days.

So I encourage you to give these grain-free basics a try. Once you see how simple they are, you'll wonder why you waited so long.

Chicken Stock

This recipe appeared in my first book, *Deliciously Organic*, but it's such a staple that it needs repeating. If you've never made your own chicken stock, don't be intimidated. You place some ingredients in a pot, cover with water, turn on the stove, and walk away. Really. It's that easy.

Homemade chicken stock serves as the foundation for many recipes, and while you can find it at the store, nothing beats the real thing. A whole chicken is preferable, but a carcass works well, too. Many times I roast a chicken, serve it for dinner, then use the carcass to make broth. It's a small way to stretch your budget without sacrificing nutrition.

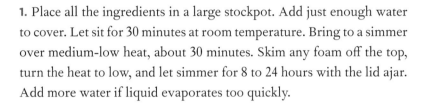

MAKES ABOUT 2 QUARTS
PREPARATION TIME: 8 to 24 hours
(almost all of this is simmering time)

One 3- to 4-pound chicken, preferably pastured

2 carrots

1 celery stalk

1 large bunch of flat-leaf parsley

2 bay leaves

1 garlic head, cut in half

1 large onion, unpeeled, cut into quarters

2 tablespoons Celtic sea salt

1 tablespoon raw apple cider vinegar

1. Place all the ingredients in a large stockpot. Add just enough water to cover. Let sit for 30 minutes at room temperature. Bring to a simmer over medium-low heat, about 30 minutes. Skim any foam off the top, turn the heat to low, and let simmer for 8 to 24 hours with the lid ajar. Add more water if liquid evaporates too quickly.

2. Strain the broth and discard the vegetables. When the chicken is cool, remove the meat and use it in soup, a casserole, or a salad, as you wish. After the broth is cool it should gelatinize, but don't be alarmed. This is a sign that the gelatin-forming nutrients (especially the amino acids proline, glycine, and glutamine) were pulled out of the chicken. To avoid breaking down these wonderful nutrients, do not allow your stock to boil for more than a few minutes after the initial boil. The gelatin is wonderful for supporting healthy collagen formation in the skin and other areas of the body. Store in the refrigerator for 1 week or freeze for 3 months.

NOTE: Chicken stock contains many nutrients and is great to have on hand during cold and flu season. We typically drink a cup of hot chicken stock each day to help keep our immune systems strong.

Ghee

Ghee is my favorite oil to use for cooking. It can withstand high temperatures without oxidizing or smoking and lends a nice buttery, nutty flavor. It's great for sautéing at high temperatures, roasting, pan frying, and so on. Many people who are lactose intolerant can handle ghee because it's purely the butter's oil, without the milk solids. Also, if you make it with organic, pastured butter, it contains many nutrients (higher amounts of omega-3 fatty acids and conjugated linoleic acid).

The word *ghee* is from India and while it may sound fancy, it's very easy to make. All you do is put the butter in a pan over low heat, walk away for forty minutes, come back, and strain off the solids. Simple! I make a batch over the weekend, pour it into a Mason jar, and use it throughout the week.

1. Melt the butter in a medium saucepan over low heat. Cook for 30 to 40 minutes, or until the butter has separated (you'll see a thick white film on top) and the milk solids that have sunk to the bottom are light brown. (While the butter is cooking, it will bubble a bit.)

2. Place a cheesecloth in a sieve over a medium bowl. Pour the melted butter through the cheesecloth and discard the solids. Store the ghee in a glass jar at room temperature (because the milk solids are removed, the oil is safe to store at room temperature) or in the refrigerator indefinitely.

MAKES ABOUT 2 CUPS
PREPARATION TIME: 45 minutes

1 pound unsalted butter

Ranch Dressing

Homemade ranch dressing takes minutes to prepare and is free of any unwanted preservatives and sugars. It keeps in the fridge for a week or two and is great for dipping.

MAKES 1¼ CUPS

PREPARATION TIME: 10 minutes

¼ cup buttermilk

½ cup homemade or good quality mayonnaise

½ cup sour cream

½ teaspoon dried dill

½ teaspoon dried parsley

½ teaspoon dried chives

1 teaspoon garlic powder

1 teaspoon fresh lemon juice

¼ teaspoon Celtic sea salt, or more to taste

Whisk all the ingredients in a small bowl until smooth. Adjust salt to taste. Refrigerate in an airtight container for about 1 week.

PALEO/DAIRY-FREE ADAPTATION: Use canned coconut milk plus 1 teaspoon lemon juice in place of the buttermilk. Use Savory Cashew "Cheese" (page 264) in place of the sour cream.

Homemade Nut Butter

Nut butters are easy to make at home and can be more nutritious than the store-bought variety. After the nuts have been properly soaked and dehydrated, just throw them in the food processor or a powerful blender and blend until creamy.

Pour the nuts and coconut oil into the bowl of a food processor and process until smooth, 10 to 13 minutes (you'll need to stop the processor occasionally to scrape down the sides). Spoon the nut butter into a jar and store in the refrigerator for up to 6 weeks.

NOTE: You can add maple syrup, coconut oil, spices, or even blend different nuts to create your own signature nut butter. My personal favorite is 2 cups pecans, ¾ cup coconut oil, ¼ cup raw honey, 1 teaspoon Celtic sea salt, and ½ teaspoon pure vanilla extract. When chilled, it tastes like cookie dough.

MAKES ABOUT 2 CUPS

PREPARATION TIME: 15 minutes

4 cups soaked and dehydrated nuts of your choice (almonds, cashews, pecans, and so on, see page 276)

1 tablespoon coconut oil

Sauerkraut

This recipe comes from my friend Winnie, who writes the lovely blog Healthy Green Kitchen. Winnie has a degree in naturopathic medicine and her blog showcases hundreds of healthy recipes. Winnie is quite the expert when it comes to fermenting and making sauerkraut, so I asked if she would share her recipe.

We usually associate sauerkraut with hot dogs, but when prepared properly it's a powerhouse food. Traditionally fermented sauerkraut contains millions of lactobacilli (good bacteria) that help keep our immune system strong. While you can purchase probiotics at the store, DIY saurkraut is easy, cheap, and more powerful than any pill. It may sound intimidating, but it's really simple to make. Just a few ingredients, salt, and a bit of muscle to pound out the juices—that's it!

MAKES 1 QUART

PREPARATION TIME: 4 to 5 days

1 small to medium cabbage (approximately 2 pounds), cored and finely shredded (a food processor is great for this, but you can also do it by hand)

1 green apple, finely shredded (optional, but it provides a nice sweetness)

2 teaspoons caraway seeds

2 tablespoons Celtic sea salt

1. In a large nonmetal bowl, toss the cabbage with the shredded apple, caraway seeds, and salt. Cover the bowl with a clean cloth and let the cabbage mixture rest for about an hour. (The cabbage will begin to wilt as the salt draws out the water.) Spoon the cabbage into a sterilized, quart-size, wide-mouth Mason jar. As you do, press down firmly with a meat pounder (the back of a wooden spoon will also work). Press hard as you pack the cabbage into the jar so that the juices come to the top of the cabbage. The cabbage should be packed very tight; stop adding more when there's an inch of headspace left. Be sure to leave a bit of room in case the sauerkraut expands while it is lacto-fermenting. (I skipped this step once and had sauerkraut juice trickling down the shelves of my pantry.)

2. Cover tightly and keep for 4 days to 2 weeks at room temperature in a dark, cool space (I keep the jars in the back of the pantry). After 4 days, the brine will be bubbly and the sauerkraut tangy. If you want a stronger flavor, continue to ferment. Transfer the sauerkraut to the refrigerator for long-term storage: The flavor improves over time.

Flavored Kombucha

Kombucha is a sweet, fermented, effervescent tea full of probiotics and properties that stimulate the liver to discard toxins. It's much more economical to make kombucha at home than buy it in stores. I've been making it for a couple of years now and the whole family loves it. I started experimenting with flavored kombucha to mix things up and found it was really quite simple to make. Instead of adding the flavored tea at the end, I like to add it at the beginning. Our favorite flavored tea is hibiscus, so I've been adding ¼ cup dried hibiscus to the hot water along with the other tea bags. It gives the tea a pretty pink color and wonderful flavor. It's very important to use filtered water in this recipe. If you don't have a water filter, such as a reverse osmosis filter, that can remove chlorine and other impurities, it's best to purchase a bottle of filtered water, such as Aquafina, at the grocery store. This recipe is adapted from Sally Fallon's book *Nourishing Traditions*, which I consider to be the bible of unprocessed, nourishing cooking.

MAKES ABOUT 3 QUARTS
PREPARATION TIME: 6 to 9 days

3 quarts filtered water

1 cup organic white sugar (evaporated cane crystals) (see Note)

4 organic green tea bags

¼ cup dried hibiscus loose-leaf tea (or your favorite loose-leaf tea, such as oolong or green tea)

½ cup kombucha from a previous culture (or bottled kombucha)

1 kombucha scoby (symbiotic culture of bacteria and yeast) or starter culture (see Note)

1. Bring the water to a boil in a large pot over medium-high heat. Add the sugar and stir until dissolved. Remove from the heat and add the green tea bags and loose-leaf tea. Steep the tea until the water has completely cooled. Remove the tea bags and pour the cooled liquid through a sieve (to remove the loose-leaf tea) into a 4-quart or larger glass bowl (not plastic). Stir in the kombucha and place the scoby on top. Cover loosely with a clean cloth or towel and transfer to a warm, dark place. Let the mixture sit for 6 to 9 days (I've found that in the warmer months, 7 days is perfect. In the colder months, I let it ferment for at least 8 or 9 days).

2. When the mixture is ready, the scoby will have grown a spongy pancake that will be lying on the top of the tea. The tea should be slightly sour and fizzy. Remove the scoby and store it in a glass container for up to 4 months in the refrigerator until you're ready to use it again. (After your first time making a batch of kombucha, the scoby that floats on top of the tea will have grown a second spongy pancake. This can be used to make other batches, or you can give it away to a friend.) Pour the kombucha into glass jars or a pitcher with a tight-fitting lid. Store in the refrigerator.

3. The kombucha will stay fresh in the refrigerator for about 2 weeks. If it loses some of its effervescence, I add a bit of sparkling water.

NOTE: While I don't use white sugar in my cooking or baking, the experts over at Cultures for Health say it's required for kombucha and a substitute should not be used. During fermentation, the white sugar reacts with the tea and kombucha culture to produce acetic, lactic, and glucuronic acid. This entire process creates this healthy fermented beverage. When the kombucha is fermented and ready to drink, the total sugar count is about 2 grams per cup.

NOTE: A scoby can be purchased at various stores online, as well as Williams-Sonoma (see Resources section, page 283).

Homemade Nut Milk

Most nut milks sold in stores are full of preservatives, additives, and added sugars, so I prefer to make them myself. All that's required is nuts, water, and a bit of unrefined sweetener if you choose. I've tried this recipe with almonds, pecans, and cashews and each version turned out beautifully. If you're looking for a rich, creamy milk, cashew is a good option. For a milk that's a bit more like skim milk, then pecan or almond is a good choice. This recipe is merely a guide. You can change the measurements or sweeteners to come up with your favorite combination.

MAKES ABOUT 2 CUPS
PREPARATION TIME: 8 hours
(almost all of this is soaking time)

1 cup raw nuts

1 teaspoon Celtic sea salt

Sweetener of your choice: dates, maple syrup, raw honey, stevia, etc. (optional)

Place the nuts, salt, and 2 cups water in a medium bowl. Gently stir to dissolve the salt. Let sit for 8 hours. Drain and rinse the nuts. Place the nuts in a blender and cover with 2 cups fresh water and the sweetener of your choice (if using). Blend for 2 minutes. Drain the mixture through cheesecloth or a fine-mesh sieve (see Note). Store the nut milk in the refrigerator for up to 5 days.

NOTE: The leftover nut meal can be added to smoothies, tossed into a batch of granola, or spread out on a baking sheet lined with unbleached parchment paper and dried in the oven (at 170°F, or as low as your oven will go, for about 4 hours) for use as nut flour in baked goods.

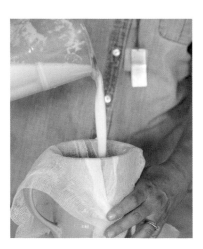

"Riced" Cauliflower

It sounds odd, but when cauliflower is cut into tiny pieces and stirred in with other ingredients, it's amazing how much it tastes like rice. I use this as a substitute for all rice dishes and the family loves it! I have many beloved family dishes that feature rice as the main ingredient. To use chopped cauliflower instead, I prepare the other ingredients in a recipe first, then add the "rice" at the end of cooking and toss until hot. For an example, see my recipe for Bacon, Mushroom, and Chard "Rice" Bowl (page 126).

Cut the cauliflower into 2-inch pieces. Place half the cauliflower in the food processor and pulse for seven or eight 1-second pulses, or until the cauliflower pieces are about the size of grains of rice. Pour into a medium bowl. Repeat with the remaining cauliflower.

SERVES 4

PREPARATION TIME: 5 minutes

1 large head of cauliflower

Savory Cashew "Cheese"

I totally turned up my nose the first time I heard about a nut "cheese," but I have to say, when it's baked in a dish like lasagna, it tastes exactly like ricotta cheese. It's a great dairy-free alternative for many dishes. It's important to soak the cashews overnight to help release the phytic acid. This will ensure proper digestion. The cheese can be stored in an airtight container in the refrigerator for one week.

MAKES ABOUT 2 CUPS
PREPARATION TIME: 10 minutes

1½ cups cashews, soaked overnight and drained
2 tablespoons fresh lemon juice
1½ tablespoons nutritional yeast
1 garlic clove
1 teaspoon Celtic sea salt

Place all the ingredients and ⅓ cup water in the bowl of a food processor or blender. Process for 3 to 4 minutes, or until smooth. You'll need to stop the processor a few times to scrape down the sides with a spatula. Then continue to process to ensure a creamy texture.

Sweet Cashew "Cheese"

Here's a great replacement for cream cheese in sweet recipes. It's simple to prepare and can be stored in the refrigerator in an airtight container for up to one week.

Place all the ingredients in the bowl of a food processor or blender. Process for 3 to 4 minutes, or until smooth. You'll need to stop the processor a few times to scrape down the sides with a spatula. Then continue to process to ensure a creamy texture.

MAKES ABOUT 3 CUPS

PREPARATION TIME: 5 minutes

1½ cups cashews, soaked overnight and drained

²/₃ cup canned coconut milk

²/₃ cup raw honey

²/₃ cup coconut oil

1 tablespoon Pure Vanilla Extract (page 274)

Having a supply of about twelve Mason jars on hand is a great way to store some of the staple recipes in this chapter. Mason jars can be found at most grocery stores or thrift stores for a minimal price. I also save the glass jars from purchased pickles or jams. The smaller jars are nice to have on hand for storing smaller portions of things like cashew cheese and baking powder.

Grain-Free Bread

Here's a bread that can be used for sandwiches or toast or served as a nice side at dinner. The pureed cashews and unflavored gelatin help add structure. The bread uses eight egg whites, so save the yolks in a jar and use them to make a pudding (page 190) or ice cream (page 208). I store the bread wrapped in a large piece of unbleached parchment paper in an airtight container for up to two days at room temperature or for four to five days in the refrigerator.

MAKES ONE 7½ X 4½-INCH LOAF
PREPARATION TIME: 1½ hours
(almost all of this is baking or soaking time)

Unsalted butter for the pan

½ cup cashews, soaked overnight and drained

8 large egg whites

1½ cups almond flour

3 tablespoons coconut flour

¾ teaspoon unflavored grass-fed gelatin

½ teaspoon Celtic sea salt

1½ teaspoons baking soda

4 tablespoons (½ stick) unsalted butter or coconut oil, melted

1 tablespoon raw honey (I use clover)

2 teaspoons raw apple cider vinegar

1. Place the cashews and ¼ cup water in a small bowl and let soak for 30 minutes.

2. Preheat the oven to 350°F and adjust the rack to the middle position. Butter a 7½ x 4½-inch glass loaf pan.

3. Pour the cashews and water into the bowl of a food processor and add the egg whites. Blend until smooth, scraping down the sides a few times to make sure all the cashews are pureed. Add the almond flour, coconut flour, gelatin, salt, baking soda, butter, honey, and vinegar and process until smooth.

4. Pour the batter into the buttered loaf pan and bake for 45 to 50 minutes, or until golden brown and a toothpick inserted in the center comes out clean. Cool for 10 minutes. Run a knife around the outer edges, invert the bread onto a cooling rack, and remove it from the loaf pan.

PALEO/DAIRY-FREE ADAPTATION: Use coconut oil in place of the butter.

Grain-Free Pie Crust

This is the perfect crust to use for any pie or tart recipe, such as the pecan pie on page 218. Omit the coconut sugar and you have a buttery crust for a quiche or savory pie.

MAKES ONE 9-INCH CRUST

PREPARATION TIME: 45 minutes
(most of this is chilling time)

2 cups almond flour

¼ cup coconut flour

½ teaspoon unflavored grass-fed gelatin

¼ teaspoon Celtic sea salt

1 teaspoon coconut sugar

8 tablespoons (1 stick) cold unsalted butter, cut into tablespoons

Place the almond flour, coconut flour, gelatin, salt, and coconut sugar in the bowl of a food processor and pulse 2 or 3 times to combine. Add the butter and pulse for eight 1-second pulses, then leave the processor on until the dough forms a ball, about 30 seconds. Press the dough over the bottom and up the sides of a 9-inch pie plate or tart pan. Refrigerate for at least 30 minutes before baking or as required in your recipe.

PALEO/DAIRY-FREE ADAPTATION: Use 5 tablespoons frozen palm shortening, cut into tablespoons, in place of butter. Add 1 egg yolk to the dough after the eight 1-second pulses.

NOTE: Almond flour crusts have a tendency to burn, so it's best to use a pie shield or a bit of foil around the edges to ensure even baking.

Thick, Homemade Yogurt

Homemade yogurt is one of life's little treats. My daughters both love yogurt, but they especially prefer our homemade recipe. The addition of grass-fed gelatin makes the yogurt thick and creamy. While I don't like having lots of extra gadgets in my kitchen, a yogurt maker has proven to be very helpful. I make a batch every few days and keep it on hand for a quick breakfast or snack.

Pour the milk into a medium saucepan over medium heat and heat it to 115°F. Remove the milk from the heat. While whisking, slowly pour in the gelatin and continue to whisk until dissolved. Cool the mixture to 110°F. Whisk in the yogurt. Pour the mixture into the glass yogurt cups and put them into the yogurt maker. Incubate at 110°F for 6 hours. Chill completely.

PALEO/DAIRY-FREE ADAPTATION: Use canned coconut milk in place of the whole milk.

NOTE. For a little variation, stir in a teaspoon of vanilla or almond extract after you've whisked in the yogurt. The extract adds a nice, subtle flavor.

MAKES ABOUT 4 CUPS
PREPARATION TIME: 6½ hours

4 cups whole milk

1¾ teaspoons unflavored grass-fed gelatin

3 tablespoons yogurt from a previous culture (or packaged whole yogurt without preservatives or added sugars)

Whipped Coconut Milk

When canned coconut milk is cold, the cream rises to the top. When this cream is skimmed off it can be whipped and used in a variety of dishes in place of traditional whipped cream.

Some coconut milk brands don't whip well; I recommend using Native Forest or Natural Value brand. Also, it's very important to refrigerate the coconut milk for twenty-four hours before whipping.

MAKES ABOUT 8 OUNCES WHIPPED COCONUT MILK

PREPARATION TIME: 5 minutes

One 14-ounce can coconut milk (Native Forest or Natural Value brand), chilled for 24 hours

Honey, maple syrup, or Pure Vanilla Extract (page 274), as desired

1. Place a mixing bowl in the freezer for 30 minutes. Open the can of coconut milk and carefully skim the cream off the top (it will be about half the contents of the can). Place the cream in the chilled mixing bowl along with honey, maple syrup, or vanilla extract, as desired.

2. Whip with a mixer until soft peaks form. Save the extra coconut milk left in the can and add it to your morning smoothie.

Dairy-Free Icing

Here's a great option for those of you who need a dairy-free alternative for frosting cakes and cookies. The recipe comes from my sweet friend Kelly Smith, who blogs at the Nourishing Home. It's a fun option to have for the kids, especially during the holidays—you can even mix in natural vegetable dyes to make colored frosting. It makes enough to frost a two-layer cake (page 204); half the recipe will ice a batch of Cut-Out or Slice-and-Bake Cookies (page 248).

1. Combine the gelatin and ¼ cup water in a small bowl. Set aside.

2. In a medium saucepan over medium heat, stir together the coconut butter, coconut cream, honey, and vanilla. Heat until melted and smooth. Whisk in the gelatin mixture until dissolved, about 30 seconds.

3. Pour the icing mixture into a medium bowl, cover, and refrigerate for 3 hours or up to 2 days.

4. Using the whisk attachment on a standing mixer, whip the icing for 3 minutes, until fluffy. You can refrigerate the frosting in an airtight container for up to 3 days.

MAKES 4 CUPS
PREPARATION TIME: 3½ hours
(most of this is chilling time)

1 teaspoon unflavored, grass-fed gelatin

2 cups Coconut Butter (page 273)

2 cups coconut cream (the thick coconut cream that rises to the top of a can of coconut milk), about 2 cans

½ cup plus 1 tablespoon raw honey

1 teaspoon Pure Vanilla Extract (page 274)

Grain-Free Baking Powder

Most commercial baking powder is made with cornstarch, so if you're avoiding grains, you'll need to make it at home. Luckily it uses only a few ingredients, and you can make a large batch and store it in an airtight container for up to six months. As with commercial baking powder, homemade loses its effectiveness over time, so halve the recipe if you don't use baking powder often.

MAKES 2 CUPS
PREPARATION TIME: 5 minutes

½ **cup baking soda**
½ **cup cream of tartar (see Note)**
1 **cup arrowroot flour**

Place all the ingredients in a small mixing bowl and stir until combined. Store in an airtight container.

NOTE: I purchase cream of tartar from Amazon or Frontier Herbs, since the bottles in the store contain only about ¼ cup.

Coconut Butter

Coconut butter is coconut that is ground in a food processor or blender until it has a smooth, buttery consistency. It's great as a spread on toast or as the foundation for a glaze on a cake. You can also mix it with other nut butters and a bit of sweetener for a nice snack. Making coconut butter at home is easy, and will save you quite a bit of money.

Place the coconut in the bowl of a food processor or high-speed blender. Process on high for 15 minutes, or until the coconut becomes a smooth butter. You'll need to stop the processor and scrape down the sides every so often. Store in an airtight container for up to 1 month.

MAKES 1½ CUPS
PREPARATION TIME: 15 minutes

4 cups unsweetened flaked coconut

Pure Vanilla Extract

Most vanilla extract sold in stores isn't a pure product. Many brands contain added sugars and caramel coloring. Vanilla extract is very easy to make at home and requires hardly any hands-on work. I always shop online for the vanilla beans, as the ones in stores can be quite pricey—check out the Resources section on page 283. Homemade also makes for a sweet gift during the holidays, so plan ahead and make a few batches in October!

MAKES 1½ CUPS

PREPARATION TIME: 5 minutes to assemble, plus 2 months to infuse

10 vanilla beans

1½ cups good-quality vodka (organic preferred)

Place the vanilla beans in a glass jar and pour the vodka over the beans. Screw the lid on tight and store in a dark, cool place (my pantry is about 75°F throughout the year). Let the vanilla extract sit for 2 months. Shake the bottle before each use. As you use up the vanilla, you can add more vodka to make the beans go further.

> You can also use this method to create homemade flavored vodka! I like to use a cup or so of fresh berries in the summertime—cherries and strawberries are especially fun because they turn the liquid red. Dry ingredients such as cinnamon sticks and cacao beans are also nice to infuse into the vodka. And exact measurements aren't really necessary. Just play with the combinations and have fun.

Sweetened Condensed Milk

As any home baker knows, sweetened condensed milk opens the door to all sorts of gooey, sweet desserts. But it's one of those ingredients I thought I'd never be able to use again. I tried countless versions in my kitchen, patiently waiting for the cream and honey to thicken, and then one day—voilà—it worked. Hallelujah! It takes quite a bit of time, but really all you do is pour two ingredients in a saucepan, turn the heat to low, and forget about it for three hours. There's not much to it.

This recipe can be used to replace one 14-ounce can of sweetened condensed milk.

Stir together the coconut milk and honey in a heavy medium saucepan and heat over medium-low heat until just simmering. Turn the heat to low (if you have a burner plate or flame tamer, here's a good opportunity to use it). Let the mixture cook slowly for about 3 hours, until reduced to about 1½ cups (I check on the mixture every once in a while to make sure it's not burning or simmering too rapidly). Pour into a glass jar or bowl, cover tightly, and refrigerate (it will continue to thicken as it cools). It will keep in the refrigerator for 1 week.

MAKES 1½ CUPS
PREPARATION TIME: 3 hours
(almost all of this is simmering time)

2½ cups canned coconut milk
⅓ cup raw honey

Soaked and Dehydrated Nuts and Seeds

Raw nuts and seeds contain phytic acid, an enzyme inhibitor (see page 7), and it's best to release the phytic acid to ensure proper digestion. Soaking them overnight in warm water and sea salt is an easy and effective method that takes only a few minutes of hands-on work. I like to make large batches and store them in glass jars in the pantry so I have them on hand for a quick snack or a topping for salads and yogurt.

MAKES 2 CUPS

PREPARATION TIME: 48 hours

4 cups nuts or seeds (pecans, almonds, sunflower seeds, pumpkin seeds, and so on)

1 tablespoon Celtic sea salt

1. Pour the nuts and salt into a large bowl and cover with warm water. Stir the mixture to dissolve the salt. Let sit at room temperature overnight, or up to 24 hours. Drain.

2. Spread the soaked and drained nuts on a baking sheet lined with unbleached parchment paper (the paper is an important step so the nuts don't stick to the pan). Bake at 170°F, or as low as your oven will go, for 8 to 10 hours, until crispy.

Savory Crepes

These savory crepes make a fantastic stand-in for soft tacos or a wrap for meats and cheeses.

1. To make the crepe batter, place the eggs, coconut milk, coconut flour, butter, and salt in a blender and blend until smooth. Add the cilantro and parsley and pulse 5 times, until the herbs are finely chopped (if you pulse too many times, the herbs will grind up too finely and the batter will become green). Refrigerate the batter for at least 1 hour or up to 8 hours.

2. Heat a 6-inch skillet over medium heat. Place a small pat of ghee on the pan and swirl to coat. Pour 2 tablespoons of the batter onto the middle of the pan and swirl to spread evenly. Cook until the bottom is just turning golden brown, about 30 seconds. Using a spatula, flip the crepe and cook for 10 seconds on the other side. Transfer the crepe to a baking sheet and repeat to make the rest of the crepes.

NOTE: The crepes freeze very well. Store in an airtight container in the freezer for up to two months.

MAKES ABOUT 16 CREPES
PREPARATION TIME: 30 minutes, plus 1 hour chilling time

6 large eggs

1 cup canned coconut milk

¼ cup coconut flour

3 tablespoons unsalted butter or coconut oil, melted

½ teaspoon Celtic sea salt

2 tablespoons chopped fresh cilantro

2 tablespoons chopped fresh parsley

¼ cup ghee or coconut oil

Bacon Mayonnaise

Sounds indulgent, right? Using bacon fat in place of olive oil takes mayonnaise to a whole new level. It's a great condiment for sandwiches and wraps or for drizzling over a grilled steak and vegetables.

MAKES ABOUT 1 CUP
PREPARATION TIME: 10 minutes

2 large egg yolks

1 tablespoon fresh lemon juice

½ teaspoon Dijon mustard

½ teaspoon Celtic sea salt

¾ cup bacon fat, melted and cooled

Whisk the egg yolks, lemon juice, Dijon, and salt in a medium bowl for 30 seconds, until creamy. Very slowly, add the bacon fat, whisking constantly until the liquid becomes very thick. (make sure the bacon fat is liquid but not hot, so the mayonnaise will emulsify). The mayonnaise keeps in the refrigerator for 1 week.

NOTE: If you don't have access to good, pastured bacon fat, you can substitute a light olive oil (extra-virgin olive oil will have too strong a flavor for this recipe).

Quick Homemade Ketchup

My kids love ketchup, but I'm not fond of the processed sweeteners and other preservatives that are often found in the jarred variety. This is a quick and easy recipe from my friend Heather, who writes the fun and uplifting blog Mommypotamus. Filled with health tips and recipes, it's one of my favorites. The ketchup will keep in the refrigerator for about a week, but in our house it's usually gone in a matter of hours!

Whisk together all the ingredients in a medium saucepan. Bring to a boil over medium-high heat, then lower the heat to a simmer and cook for 10 minutes.

MAKES ABOUT 2 CUPS

PREPARATION TIME: 10 minutes

1½ cups tomato paste

½ cup maple syrup

½ cup plus 2 tablespoons raw apple cider vinegar

2 tablespoons onion powder

1 teaspoon Celtic sea salt

Scant ¼ teaspoon allspice

Dandelion and Chicory Root Tea (Coffee Substitute)

As much as we all love coffee, the truth is, it's just not very healthy. It's a very acidic drink that can wreak havoc on the adrenal glands (which produce hormones that help us deal with stress). Coffee was the hardest thing for me to give up on my journey to better health. First I slowly switched to organic decaf, and then I started drinking this dandelion and chicory root tea. It's a rich, dark drink that's as close to coffee as you can get. I like to drink it with a splash of fresh cream and a teaspoon of honey. It can be brewed in a drip coffee maker or a French press. I mix the dandelion and chicory root in large batches and store it in a glass jar in the pantry.

MAKES 1 QUART
PREPARATION TIME: 5 minutes

2 teaspoons roasted dandelion (see Note)
2 teaspoons roasted chicory root

Place the dandelion and chicory root in the filter of a coffee maker. Add 1 quart water and brew according to the manufacturer's directions. Serve with cream and honey if desired.

NOTE: I purchase the roasted dandelion and chicory root in large bags from Amazon.

universal conversion chart

Oven temperature equivalents

250°F = 120°C

275°F = 135°C

300°F = 150°C

325°F = 160°C

350°F = 180°C

375°F = 190°C

400°F = 200°C

425°F = 220°C

450°F = 230°C

475°F = 240°C

500°F = 260°C

Measurement equivalents

Measurements should always be level unless directed otherwise

⅛ teaspoon = 0.5 ml

¼ teaspoon = 1 ml

½ teaspoon = 2 ml

1 teaspoon = 5 ml

1 tablespoon = 3 teaspoons = ½ fluid ounce = 15 ml

2 tablespoons = ⅛ cup = 1 fluid ounce = 30 ml

4 tablespoons = ¼ cup = 2 fluid ounces = 60 ml

5⅓ tablespoons = ⅓ cup = 3 fluid ounces = 80 ml

8 tablespoons = ½ cup = 4 fluid ounces = 120 ml

10⅔ tablespoons = ⅔ cup = 5 fluid ounces = 160 ml

12 tablespoons = ¾ cup = 6 fluid ounces = 180 ml

16 tablespoons = 1 cup = 8 fluid ounces = 240 ml

resources

Meat

Primal Pastures: www.PrimalPastures.com

Tendergrass Farms: www.TendergrassFarms.com

U.S. Wellness Meats: www.grasslandbeef.com

Milk

Real Milk (to find fresh, raw, organic milk in your area): www.RealMilk.com

Organic Pastures: www.OrganicPastures.com

Organic Valley Grassmilk: www.OrganicValley.com

Coconut Milk

Native Forest Organic Coconut Milk: www.NativeForest.com

Wilderness Family Naturals Organic Coconut Milk: www.WildernessFamilyNaturals.com

Butter

Kerrygold Butter: www.Kerrygold.com

Organic Pastures Raw Butter: www.OrganicPastures.com

Organic Valley Pasture Butter: www.OrganicValley.com

Yogurt

Stonyfield Organic Whole Milk Yogurt: www.Stonyfield.com

Straus Organic Yogurt: www.StrausFamilyCreamery.com

Trader Joe's Whole Milk Organic Yogurt: www.TraderJoes.com

Sour Cream

Straus Organic Sour Cream: www.StrausFamilyCreamery.com

Fats and Oils

Bariani Extra-Virgin Olive Oil: www.Radiantlifecatalog.com

Tropical Traditions coconut oil and palm shortening: www.TropicalTraditions.com

U.S. Wellness Meats beef tallow: www.GrassLandBeef.com

Wilderness Family Naturals coconut oil and olive oil: www.WildernessFamilyNaturals.com

Almond Flour

Honeyville Farms: www.Honeyville.com

Coconut Flour

Bob's Red Mill: www.BobsRedMill.com

Nuts.com: www.Nuts.com

Tropical Traditions: www.TropicalTraditions.com

Sprouted Bean Flours

To Your Health Sprouted Flour:
www.OrganicSproutedFlour.net

Spices

Mountain Rose Herbs:
www.MountainRoseHerbs.com

Frontier: www.FrontierCoop.com

Starter Cultures for Kombucha, Homemade Cheese, Yogurt, and So On

Cultures for Health: www.CulturesforHealth.com

Williams-Sonoma: www.Williams-Sonoma.com

Grass-Fed Gelatin

Bernard Jensen: www.BernardJensen.com

Great Lakes Unflavored Gelatin:
www.GreatLakesGelatin.com

Fermented Tamari

Gold Mine Natural Food Co., Ohsawa Organic
Gluten-Free Tamari:
www.GoldMineNaturalFoods.com

Fermented Sauerkraut

Bubbies: www.Bubbies.com

Eden Foods Organic Sauerkraut:
www.EdenFoods.com

Farmhouse Culture: www.FarmHouseCulture.com

Gold Mine Natural Foods Co.:
www.GoldMineNaturalFoods.com

Maple Syrup

Coombs Family Farm:
www.CoombsFamilyFarms.com

NOW Foods: www.NowFoods.com

Tropical Traditions: www.TropicalTraditions.com

Raw Honey

Really Raw Honey: www.ReallyRawHoney.com

Tropical Traditions: www.TropicalTraditions.com

Y. S. Eco Bee Farms Honey: www.YSOrganic.com

Maple Sugar

Coombs Family Farms:
www.CoombsFamilyFarms.com

Trader Joe's: www.TraderJoes.com

Coconut Sugar

Tropical Traditions: www.TropicalTraditions.com

Wilderness Family Naturals:
www.WildernessFamilyNaturals.com

Sucanat

(Some brands process their Sucanat in a factory
with wheat, so be sure to read the label before
purchasing.)

Wholesome Sweeteners:
www.WholesomeSweeteners.com

Vanilla Extract

Rodelle's Organic Vanilla Extract:
www.Rodellekitchen.com

Pickles

Bubbies: www.Bubbies.com

Coconut Aminos

Coconut Secret Coconut Aminos:
www.CoconutSecret.com

Paleo/Grain-Free Bread and Wraps

Coconut Wraps from The Pure Wraps:
www.ThePureWraps.com

Paleo Bread from Julian Bakery:
www.JulianBakery.com

Paleo Wraps from Julian Bakery:
www.JulianBakery.com

WEB SITES WITH GREAT DISCOUNTS

Amazon: www.Amazon.com

Azure Standard: www.azurestandard.com

Tropical Traditions: www.TropicalTraditions.com

Vitacost: www.Vitacost.com

COOKWARE AND BAKEWARE

Enameled Cookware

Le Creuset: www.LeCreuset.com

Lodge: www.LodgeMFG.com

Staub: www.StaubUSA.com

Stainless Steel Cookware

All-Clad: www.AllClad.com

Le Creuset: www.LeCreuset.com

Baking Dishes, Pans, and So On

Pyrex 9-inch cake pans and casserole dishes:
www.Pyrex.com

Simax glass bundt pan: www.MightyNest.com

Stainless steel muffin pans and baking sheets:
www.MightyNest.com

Favorite Online Stores for Cookware, Bakeware, Lunch Gear, and Other Kitchen Goods

Amazon: www.Amazon.com

Mighty Nest: www.MightyNest.com

Sur La Table: www.SurLaTable.com

Williams-Sonoma: www.Williams-Sonoma.com

FURTHER READING

Bowden, Jonny, and Steven Sinatra. *The Great Cholesterol Myth: Why Lowering Your Cholesterol Won't Prevent Heart Disease—and the Statin-Free Plan That Will.* Massachusetts: Fair Winds Press, 2012.

Campbell-McBride, Natasha. *Gut and Psychology Syndrome: Natural Treatment for Autism, Dyspraxia, A.D.D., Dyslexia, A.D.H.D., Depression, Schizophrenia.* United Kingdom: Medinform Publishing, 2010.

Davis, William. *Wheat Belly.* Pennsylvania: Rodale, 2011.

Enig, Mary. *Eat Fat, Lose Fat.* New York: Plume, 2006.

Fallon, Sally. *Nourishing Traditions: The Cookbook That Challenges Politically Correct Nutrition and the Diet Dictocrats.* Indiana: New Trends Publishing, Inc., 2003.

Fallon, Sally. *The Nourishing Traditions Book of Baby and Child Care Nutrition and the Diet.* Indiana: New Trends Publishing, Inc., 2013.

Price, Weston. *Nutrition and Physical Degeneration.* California: Price Pottenger Nutrition, 2009.

Shanahan, Catherine. *Deep Nutrition: Why Your Genes Need Traditional Food.* Hawaii: Big Box Books, 2008.

Taubes, Gary. *Why We Get Fat: And What to Do About It.* New York: Anchor, 2011.

Williams, Louisa. *Radical Medicine: Cutting-Edge Natural Therapies That Treat the Root Causes of Disease.* Vermont: Healing Arts Press, 2011.

many thanks

I first have to thank my Lord and Savior for allowing me to walk through the trials and come out stronger on the other end. I truly learned the meaning of how to "give thanks in all things." Life is so much better when I give thanks for everything in my path.

Pete, Hannah, and Abby—thank you for walking with me through the health issues and making our grain-free journey a joyful experience. Pete, you are such an inspiration and a man of solid character. You always have grounded advice when I need it most. Hannah and Abby—thank you for the encouragement and understanding, especially when we moved cross-country and set up our house, and then I was swamped with writing this book. Having you in the kitchen with me was such a joy!

Thank you to my editor, Cassie Jones, for taking on this project and helping me get my story out to those who need it. You have been a blast to work with!

My agent Meg Thompson—thank you for believing in my story and mission to help others. I'm so blessed to have such a talented and passionate agent in my corner.

My life would be very different without my sweet friend and nutritionist, Kim Schuette. Your insight and support have meant the world to me these last several years.

Amy Burgess—thank you for helping me mold and craft my voice.

Karin—you were one of my only friends who stuck beside me when my health was quickly disintegrating. Thank you for all of your calls, prayers, and wise advice.

Lisa Leake—thank you for all your support and friendship. It's so nice to have a like-minded friend in the food blogging world.

My parents—thank you for teaching me the importance of integrity and hard work. Dad, you have reminded me through the years to use my trials to help others, and this book is proof of how one can turn trial into joy. Mom, cooking beside you in the kitchen for all those years was the best cooking school a girl could ask for!

Thank you, June and Tori, for your constant support and prayers and for opening up your hearts to this project.

Molly Chester—one of my dearest friends, and one of the best cooks I know. Thank you for brainstorming recipe ideas with me, listening to my worries, and always being an encouragement.

Kelly Trimble and Cole Rosenbaum—our little team of three had quite the fun down at Seagrove beach to shoot all of the personality shots. Thank you for your hard work and helping me make this project a success.

Dede Edwards and Ginny Wosak—thank you for capturing my girls in their element. You were such a joy to work with.

At William Morrow/HarperCollins, thanks to Kara Zauberman for handling all my many e-mails and helping the process go smoothly, as well as Julia Gang, Lorie Pagnozzi, Kris Tobiassen, Joyce Wong, Anna Brower, Liate Stehlik, Lynn Grady, Andy Dodds, Zea Moscone, and Tavia Kowalchuk.

index

Note: Page references in *italics* indicate photographs.